ROBERT BENEDETTI
YALE SCHOOL OF DRAMA

The Actor
At Work

PRENTICE-HALL, INC.
ENGLEWOOD CLIFFS, NEW JERSEY

The Prentice-Hall Series in Theatre and Drama
OSCAR G. BROCKETT, Consulting Editor

ROBERT L. BENEDETTI, *The Actor at Work*
CHARLOTTE KAY MOTTER, *Theatre in High School:
Planning, Teaching,
Directing*

For Dr. Robert Breen

© 1970 by Prentice-Hall, Inc. Englewood Cliffs, N.J.

Library of Congress Catalog Card Number 75-116615

Printed in the United States of America

13-003657-9

Current Printing (Last Digit)
10   9 8 7 6 5 4 3 2 1

Prentice-Hall International, Inc., *London*
Prentice-Hall of Australia, Pty. Ltd., *Sydney*
Prentice-Hall of Canada, Ltd., *Toronto*
Prentice-Hall of India Private Limited, *New Delhi*
Prentice-Hall of Japan, Inc., *Tokyo*

Acknowledgments

To Dr. Robert S. Breen of Northwestern University for his insight into the underlying relationship of social acting and stage acting, which is the foundation of this book; to Dr. John C. Edwards of the University of New Hampshire for the technique of polarization exercises; to Dr. Oscar Brockett of Indiana University for the idea to write this book, and for his generous help over the three years it took to do the job; to my colleagues at the Drama Department of Carnegie-Mellon University and its chairman Earle Gister, and to the Department of Theatre Arts at the University of Wisconsin-Milwaukee and its chairman Corliss Phillabaum, for all that they have contributed to my thinking; to Carol Egan, Jewel Walker, and Paul Draper for their thoughts about stage movement; to my many friends at the Milwaukee Repertory Theatre and their numerous suggestions; to my students who taught me about acting; to my sophomore acting class at Carnegie-Mellon University who are pictured in the illustrations. And most of all to my wife who kept me at it, and taught me to write too.

Exercises

EXERCISES FOR ONE OR TWO PEOPLE

GROUP EXERCISES

Contents

Introduction

No book, including this one, can teach you to act. It is doubtful, in fact, if anyone has ever been taught to act, or to paint, or to compose. Only the skills of art can be taught, not art itself. A good acting teacher provides a sound foundation of necessary skills and instills the discipline by which they may be mastered. He communicates to the student the bases upon which these skills may be applied. He does all this with a personal concern for the student, wishing to *liberate* and *nurture* whatever talent the student possesses. When he is being honest with himself, his greatest fear is that he stifles as many talents as he liberates.

But not even in his greatest successes can he claim to have taught the creative act itself. At his best, he has only helped the student to realize himself.

For better or for worse, then, this book presents an introductory course in acting stressing the two main areas of acting "technique": interpretation and expressiveness. In the first part of the book, which deals with expressive technique, I have taken a strongly organismic approach, drawing material from various fields (principally Gestalt psychology like that practised at Essalen, social pyschology, philosophy, linguistics, and recent experimental theatrical training programs). I have tried continually to relate the structuring of a theatrical discipline to the inherently dramatic aspects of everyday expressive behavior.

The second part of the book treats in considerable detail the techniques of textual analysis, a subject that is shockingly neglected by most training programs. For years our schools and academies have been producing actors who "play by ear," who literally can't read their music.

You may even wonder, toward the end of the book, "when is he going to get to the acting?" I'm not. Hopefully, you are. The first part is called "The Actor's Tools," and the second, "The Actor's Blueprint," because my aim is to help you understand what your job is, and to help you begin developing the skills you need to do it. But the synthesis and application of that understanding and those skills in the creative act is a complex and highly personal matter beyond the province of this book, and perhaps beyond the province of the introductory phase of an actor's training. All the world's leading training programs devote at least the first year (usually the first two) to developing skills, and they actually *restrain* the student from acting during this period.

If a student is asked to solve the problems of creating a role for performance before he possesses a firm foundation of basic technique, he will, by necessity, develop bad habits that are difficult to dislodge later. The steps from basic "skills" exercises, to scene work, to workshop performance must be taken when they will best benefit the student's development.

This book concerns itself with the first phase of this process (basic skills) and moves into the second (scene work). Limited as it is to materials appropriate to the introductory phases of a long-range training program, the book does *not* present an over-all survey of acting in the way an introductory history text might cover all major periods in a general way.

The debate between "professional" and "academic" training programs seems absurd. There is no reason why the student actor should not be prepared to earn a decent living at his craft, nor any reason why his training should therefore be restricted to the immediate demands of an artistically impoverished commercial theatre. The traditional suspicion of "professional" programs in the arts is finally being overcome in our educational institutions. The sort of conservatory environment so long enjoyed by young artists in the old world is coming to America at last. It is to the conservatory-type program that this book is directed.

Since this is, then, essentially a "skills" book, the many exercises I have included are the very heart of it. They are meant as training devices, *not* as rehearsal techniques. Their aim is to focus your awareness on various experiences and skills, as a program of self-discovery and development in graduated stages. They are not meant to provide you with an all-purpose methodology for acting. No such all-purpose methodology exists. If it did, we would stop calling acting an art, and move into some more exciting line of work.

Every play presents its own problems and demands its own solutions; moreover, every play contains the seeds that generate those solutions, if the actor is craftsman enough to apply the appropriate interpretive and expressive skills to realize them. This craftsmanship is the necessary antecedent of artistry in the creation of a synthesized and living performance.

The emerging repertory companies need actors who are stylistically versatile and who contribute to the intellectual *and* the artistic vitality of the companies to which they belong. Also, as we move fully out of the era of realistic playwriting, we find the subjectivism of old acting approaches floundering before the demands of much new writing and the revitalized classical repertory. The intuitive actor with his "own" one way of working will no longer suffice.

Throughout, I have tried to use examples to illustrate points taken from a few plays of various representative types. One of the great difficulties in teaching acting is that acting students are familiar with so few plays. If you will take time at the outset to read the following plays, from which almost all my examples are drawn, you will benefit much more from the examples themselves: Shakespeare's *King Lear* and *Romeo and Juliet*, Brecht's *Mother Courage*, Miller's *Death of a Salesman*, Albee's *Zoo Story*, and Beckett's *Endgame*.

The development of the material follows roughly the "natural" acquisition of these skills, beginning basically and simply and moving toward greater complexity and subtlety. This progression continues through the exercises, so it is important that the exercises be read as carefully as the main body of the text, even if they are not performed. They are meant, of course, to be performed, and the experiences they provide are essential to a true understanding (in the muscles as well as in the mind) of this book's point of view.

Despite the fact that these exercises are largely drawn from a type of therapeutic psychology, I must stress that this book makes no pretentions of a therapeutic or even philosophical nature. Acting is a rigorous and hard-headed discipline, and my approach is designed (and has been extensively class-tested) for efficacy alone.

There are, nevertheless, many benefits awaiting the serious young actor, none of which relate to fame and success. Descartes said that reading good books was like conversing with the greatest minds of history, minds that had distilled their experience and wisdom in their art. We who perform good plays go a step further; we actively participate in the experience of peoples, places, and ages, which have been shaped and condensed by the artistic consciousness of great playwrights. Theatre is the most human of all the arts and we, and our audience with us, can expand our humanity through our art in ways denied us by everyday life. In turn, our extended sensitivity can reveal to us the unseen and unsuspected vibrancy of the human condition, which is the raw material of all great drama.

PART ONE

The

Actor's

Tools

The Need
for
Technique

An actor creates, with his body and voice, sights and sounds
that contribute to the artistically patterned experience we call
a play.

The theatre is a physical place, and all meanings,
philosophical or psychological insights, emotions—all that may
be communicated by a play—first reach the spectator as the
physical sensations that the actor creates. These physical
sensations are the result of careful preparation. Behind them lie
careful study of the playscript and complex interpretive decisions
by the actor and his director, which are intended to express the
playwright's original conception.

But before the playwright's conception or the director's
interpretation can live, the actor must translate them into
meaningfully patterned sensations communicable to an
audience. Until this has been done, theatre can exist only on an
intellectual or literary level. The skill of the actor in creating
expressive sensations is what makes theatre a potentially full
human experience, the "liveliest" among all the arts.

The actor's job is threefold: first, he must develop his own
expressiveness, reaching deeply into his own being and creating
from his everyday feelings a highly responsive and versatile
system of reactions; second, he must develop the skills of
analysis, which will teach him to penetrate the surface of his
script and to mine its hidden riches; and third, he must master
the technical skills of the stage until he is absolutely in control

*of the theatrical environment, completely free to bring the
vitality of his responses into a creative synthesis with the detail
provided by his script and to communicate this synthesis to his
audience with the utmost effectiveness.*

*We might add to this list the one "unteachable" and essential
skill of the good actor, his "instinct" for* role-playing. *It is this
imaginative ability to put oneself in the place of a fictitious
character in the manner demanded by the form and style of the
character's play that provides the vitality of all good acting.*

*The activity of role-playing is not unique to the stage actor.
It is one of the common and necessary activities of everyday
social life. As you begin developing yourself as a stage actor,
you will find that a great deal of your skill as a social actor will
be useful. You are probably already more skillful at projecting
a semi-fictitious characterization to an audience than you might
think.*

*Around the turn of the century, the psychologist William
James suggested that our personality is a complex structure
consisting of an "I" and several "me's." Each of us has a good
many roles, or "me's," which we play in various situations.
Your roles as son or daughter, as student, as employee, and so
on, all call upon you to modify your behavior at different times,
to present yourself differently. Your sense of identity, your
"I," is your sense of continuous identity, which lies behind these
various performances and ties them together into one personality.
If you have ever been forced to perform two different social
roles at once (visits by parents to their children at college often
occasion such uncomfortable situations), you know how radically
different some of our "me's" can be from each other. Our sanity
depends, in part, on keeping our various "me's" in their proper
place and holding on to a strong sense of "I."*

*A contemporary social psychologist, Erving Goffman, has
analyzed social behavior as if it were a dramatic performance.
He finds that most of us have a highly developed ability to play
successfully the role demanded from us at each moment.*

*It does take deep skill, long training, and psychological capacity to
become a good stage actor. But this fact should not blind us to another
one: that almost anyone can quickly learn a script well enough to give
a charitable audience some sense of realness in what is being contrived*

before them. And it seems this is so because ordinary social intercourse is itself put together as a scene is put together, by the exchange of dramatically inflated actions, counteractions, and terminating replies. Scripts even in the hands of unpracticed players can come to life because life itself is a dramatically enacted thing. All the world is not, of course, a stage, but the crucial ways in which it isn't are not easy to specify. . . . The legitimate performances of everyday life are not "acted" or "put on" in the sense that the performer knows in advance just what he is going to do. . . . But . . . the incapacity of the ordinary individual to formulate in advance the movements of his eyes and body does not mean that he will not express himself through these devices in a way that is dramatized and pre-formed in his repertoire of actions. In short, we all act better than we know how.[1]

Our skill as social actors gives us a firm foundation upon which to build. But our training must be intensive and specialized. As Goffman says, anyone can quickly be taught to give some sense of life to a part, but that is a very different thing from becoming a really good stage actor. As a social actor, you have practiced for years just to portray yourself. The stage actor must give artistically intensified performances of a whole range of extraordinary characters, usually quite different from himself, and "living" in very different worlds. The good actor is rarely "himself" on stage; he has put himself into his character rather than forcing the character to conform to his own habitual manner of expression and thought.

We have already named the three basic skills necessary to you as an actor: physical and vocal mastery, analytical insight into your text, and the ability to synthesize concepts and techniques in role-playing. Each of these skills is dependent upon the other. Without any one, the other two are useless. The true actor strives to achieve all, and disciplines himself in each area.

Here in the training program we can start you off by providing you with some of the tools you need to become an actor. We can help you work on your voice, on your bodily expressiveness; we can help you develop an intelligent and sensitive relationship to the plays you perform; we can teach you techniques of concentration and role-playing. All this will take time. Your formal training will barely prepare you to start

---

[1] From *The Presentation of Self in Everyday Life* by Erving Goffman. Copyright © 1959 by Erving Goffman. Reprinted by permission of Doubleday & Company, Inc.

becoming *an actor. It is very important that these "first steps"
of yours be good ones. Bad habits, shortcuts, gimmicks, and
false values are the results of impatience, and are difficult to
correct later.*

*Patience and a sense of striving together—being able to
accept the momentary failure for the sake of the long-range
success—is the attitude that the young actor must nurture. The
pressures of our educational system are against this attitude,
as is the normal desire of all of us to be "successful" right* now.
*Resist your desire to be an overnight star. Explore a variety of
approaches and experiences. Most of your explorations will
lead up blind alleys, but it is better to suffer momentary
disappointments now than to commit yourself to an approach or
an attitude that will hopelessly limit you later.*

*Discipline also involves persistence and regularity. Your
work on technical skills especially must be a* daily *affair.
Stanislavski, looking back late in his life, had this to say:*

Let someone explain to me why the violinist who plays in an orchestra
on the tenth violin must daily perform hour-long exercises or lose his
power to play? Why does the dancer work daily over every muscle in
his body? Why do the painter, the sculptor, the writer practice their art
each day and count that day lost when they do not work? And why may
the dramatic artist do nothing, spend his day in coffee houses and hope
for the gift of [inspiration] in the evening? Enough. Is this an art when
its priests speak like amateurs? There is no art that does not demand
virtuosity.[2]

You must have the patience to work each day, *to watch
techniques develop slowly and improve. Learning to act is the
development of patient, persistent self-discipline.*

*The aim in the first part of this book is to start you out on
the very long road toward the development and maintenance of
your skills. Careful decisions and the development of a serious
and disciplined working attitude at this stage of your career
will be one of the most important investments you will ever
make. The development of vocal and physical expressiveness*

---

[2]From *My Life In Art* by Constantin Stanislavski, translated by J. J. Robbins,
Copyright 1924 by Little, Brown & Co. and 1952 by Elizabeth Reynolds Hapgood. Used
with the permission of the publishers, Theatre Arts Books, New York, and Geoffrey
Bles, Ltd.

and the ability to comprehend the life of a character are skills that you will only begin to master in the early stages of your theatrical training. Moreover, these are skills you will never fully master—and this is one of the greatest joys of acting. You will never be "finished;" you will always be learning and changing. Change, especially for the artist, is necessary to continuing vitality.

Contacting Yourself

"Mister Duffy lived at a little distance from his body." This description of one of James Joyce's characters applies to most of us in our everyday lives. As actors, however, we can no more maintain this distance from our own bodies than could a violinist refuse contact with his violin.

It is not an easy task to come to grips with one's own physical existence. As one psychologist has so beautifully put it, you must "invade your own privacy." This will be the purpose of the next few lessons. While beginning to get to know yourself, it will be useful to avoid words like "subjective" and "objective," and "mind" and "body." We do not start out in life divided between a physical and an intellectual self, but as we "mature," most of us develop such a split. We begin to think about ourselves as if we had two parts, a "mind" and a "body." The actor, who must manipulate his voice and body, his thoughts and feelings in order to achieve a unified stage creation, must strive to realize that the mind and body are one and inseparable. The "mind" is an aspect of the physical body. "Mental" and "physical" are not different *kinds* of behavior, though these terms may be useful to indicate different *qualities* of behavior.

For the actor, the "concept" of a role and the "physical realization" of the role are also one and inseparable. When we say that one actor can "conceive" his role beautifully but has trouble manifesting his understanding in performance, while another actor has complete physical control but lacks adquate conception, we are really saying that each in his own way has incompletely realized the totality, the indivisible wholeness, which is essential to any living stage creation. The ideal toward which you must work is realizing a unity of conception and physicalization, and the only way for you to develop in this integrated manner is by contacting your own existence so profoundly that the distinctions between concept and realization, mental and physical, subjective and objective cease to exist.

Ultimately you hope to reach the point where even the distinction between the "senses," "emotion," and "body" cease to exist. How many times directors have said to actors, "you're not seeing with your whole body!" and "you're not feeling with your whole body!" The voice has also suffered the same sort of artificial separation from the whole body that produces it, and more often than not we could also say, "you're not *speaking* with your whole body." Once you have realized that the voice, senses, emotions, and body are integral with one another, you will see the thread that connects the words printed on the page of your script with all aspects—verbal and nonverbal—of your ultimate performance.

THE EXERCISES

There are a great many pressures upon us to avoid contact with ourselves. Considerable discipline and continual attention is necessary to overcome both our fear and our laziness: fear of the acuteness of a realization of our own naked presence, and laziness regarding the expenditure of energy necessary to achieve this realization. I can present here only a few beginning exercises, which many have found useful. They are derived from a program of therapy developed by Gestalt psychologists, and you will probably recognize some of them as similar to Yoga exercises. We need not go into the philosophical backgrounds of either Gestalt psychology or Yoga, since we use these exercises only as a starting point for a cohesive physical training program for the actor. Our interest is in what they can do for the development of our technical skills and not for any therapeutic effect they may have (though you will find that their contribution to your general well-being may be very great).

The results of these exercises are seldom immediate and can be properly measured only by their long-range effect. At first you may regard them as "silly," or at best ineffective. Such resistance toward committing yourself to a program of physical development probably springs from those same inhibitions you are attempting to overcome. You more than likely have such defenses against any public physical involvement. It is the actor's first attitudinal task to realize that he is often called upon to behave in a *private* manner within a *public* situation.

CONTACTING THE ACTUAL

You are working toward a realization of your actual being which is rare in Western culture. We need not suggest any spiritual, moral, or philosophical reasons why such an experience is desirable for an actor. It is a simple, mechanical necessity that an actor explore and extend the fullest possible range of his experience, since it is this experience that will provide him with the ultimate materials of his craft. Such a program of development, however, will inevitably have a profound impact upon you:

To reacquire the full feeling of actuality is an experience of tremendous impact, moving to the core. In the clinical situation, patients have cried out, "Suddenly I feel like jumping to the air!" And, "I'm walking, really walking!" And, "I feel so peculiar—the world is there, *really there!*" And, "I have eyes, *real eyes!*" But there is a long road . . . to such a full experience.[3]

Realizing "where you are" on stage provides a point of physical contact between you and your environment, which anchors and focuses your concentration and gives a firm basis in physical fact for the *experience* which you construct upon that reality. In this way, the *experience* which you create is made more "real," that is, more palpable, by its derivation from *your* physical actuality on stage.

RELAXATION

The first actuality with which you must come to terms is that of your own body, and the first step in contacting your body is that of relaxation. By relaxation, I do *not* mean a passive state: I mean, rather, a state in which all bodily tensions have been perfectly balanced and reduced, and in which inhibitions have been lifted. The human organism is not passive by nature: "inhibition" means literally an "in-holding." As the psychologists say, "If the inhibition is lifted, what was held in does not then passively emerge; rather, the person *actively*, eagerly brings it forth."[4]

When we speak of relaxation on stage, we mean that all *unnecessary* tensions have been removed and that the remaining tensions have been balanced. This is obvious, since only an extremely lazy actor (or a fool) could even *hope* to be truly "relaxed" at a time when he has such an important and complex job to do. The kind of relaxation that we wish for could be defined as *that state in which the actor is most ready to react to the slightest stimulus.* In other words, a state in which all inhibitions to movement or reaction have been removed.

While some of your physical tensions are vitally necessary on stage, the majority of these tensions become obstacles to your free reaction and must be removed. The energy that remains, the useful energy, must be in harmonious balance, so that you are free to move or react in any way required, without wasting energy in first overcoming inhibition. A good way of describing the relaxed actor would be to say that he is "at rest," or "waiting to move."

The first step in achieving relaxation is to identify, localize, and rid yourself of all unnecessary tensions, and your first exercise will be to inspect the tensions within your body.

[3] Frederick S. Perls, Ralph F. Hefferline, and Paul Goodman, *Gestalt Therapy* (New York: The Julien Press, 1951), p. 41. Dell Paperback, 1964.

[4] Perls, Hefferline, and Goodman, *Gestalt Therapy*, p. 22.

Exercise 1: Playing Cat

Select a comfortable position in a surrounding that is not too distracting. Do not "try to relax." Trying to relax is like trying to fall asleep—it can't be done. At best, you are trying to become aware of the tensions that prevent you from relaxing. As we shall explore later, relaxation can be achieved only as a by-product of some focus of concentration. For this exercise, our focus of concentration will be the tensions within your body. Stretch yourself out face up in an aligned position, hands at your side. Put yourself at rest by yawning and stretching.

> To see yawning and stretching at their luxurious best, watch a cat just awakening from a siesta. It arches its back, extends to the utmost legs, feet, and toes, drops its jaw, and all the while balloons itself up with air. Once it has swelled until it occupies its very maximum of space, it permits itself slowly to collapse—and then is ready for new business.[5]

Perform the role of the cat. Stretch, arch your back, extend all your limbs to their utmost, drop the jaw, wiggle the arms and hands and breathe deeply (not once but many times) each time taking in more and more air. When the yawn, the tingling in the lips, comes of its own accord, settle back onto the floor.

Now, lying in this hopefully euphoric state, pinpoint your attention on any area of your body that has failed to play the game. Perhaps it is your right hand, or the toes of your left foot, or the small of your back, or the nape of your neck, or your buttocks. Wherever tensions occur, focus the full force of your concentration upon that area. Manipulate it, attack it, until those tensions have been quelled. Continue breathing as fully as possible. Although you are not *trying* to relax, do not prevent spontaneous relaxation when it occurs. *This exercise of putting yourself at rest will be the starting point of each of the following exercises.*

THE HERE AND NOW

Relaxation is possible only as a by-product of your focus of concentration. In order to achieve realization of your actual presence on stage, your primary point of awareness must be the present moment, not the past or the future. Relaxation in the sense of being "ready to act" demands that you immerse yourself in the present instant, because it is only *now* that you *exist*. This is more difficult to achieve than would be imagined. We tend to protect ourselves from the unknown of the immediate moment

---

[5] Perls, Hefferline, and Goodman, *Gestalt Therapy*, p. 134.

by dwelling imaginatively in the past or the future. Daydreaming and wool-gathering are almost continuous processes. We rarely risk complete contact with the present: we prefer a sense of comfortable continuity, achieved by blurring the lines that separate the present from the past and future. The past, in memory, and the future, in expectation, can both be controlled by our consciousness; but the present can be met only on its own terms. Although you can never *specifically isolate* it, you can put yourself in touch with the unending *flow* of the present.

> The wish to seize the present and pin it down—to mount it, as it were, like a butterfly in a case—is doomed to failure. Actuality forever changes. In healthy persons, the feeling of actuality is steady and continuous but, like the view from a train window, the scenery is always different.[6]

Exercise 2: Here and Now

Put yourself at rest as above. Now say to yourself sentences describing your immediate awareness. For example, "Right now I am lying on the floor, I am doing exercise number two, I am making up sentences, what will I do first, my right hand is a little cold" and so on. Do this as long as you can.

How far did you go? Why did you stop where you did? Was there anything you ignored or avoided? Repeat the exercise. Go farther. After each repetition, examine your responses. Where did your awareness take you? How hard was it for you to stay completely in the present? Did you wander backward into memory, or into the future? Were your responses "physical" or "mental"? What did you avoid? Most of these exercises have no specific "end," and can remain useful indefinitely as warm-up exercises. The immediate purpose of this exercise has been more or less fulfilled when the temptation to wander into the past or the future has been so completely overcome that you can remain comfortably and effortlessly in the present.

THE BODY AS A UNIT

Full awareness and concentration on stage, so necessary to any successful performance, are possible only in the present, since your body, as a natural object, participates in the unending change and flow of time. One of the points of concentration to which you may have been led in the last exercise is the *dynamic* nature of your own existence. In the next exercise, we turn our attention to developing our sense of wholeness. It is essential for all that

---

[6] Perls, Hefferline, and Goodman, *Gestalt Therapy*, p. 33.

comes later that you begin to experience yourself as a unified organism with each part, each sensation, each experience integrated fully into the whole of your being.

Exercise 3: Sensing Wholeness

Put yourself at rest. Focus your attention on each area of your body, starting at the bottom and working your way up. Say hello to each and every toe, to the balls of your feet, to the arch, to the ankle, to your calf, to your knee, and so on. Next spend a period of time randomly focusing concentration on various areas of the body. Let your concentration skip wherever it may—from your right thigh to your left big toe and so on. Notice aches and pains and muscle tensions that you normally ignore. Do not try to relax them; simply try to become aware of their precise location. Become aware, too, of generalized responses, like skin sensations, muscle tone, and so on. Can you feel your body as a whole? Are you aware of each part in relation to the whole?

When you have worked for some time on the exercise up to this point, proceed to focus attention on combinations of things that go on in your body. What does a tension in your right arm mean for your left leg? Is there any relationship between a straining sensation in your ears and certain skin sensations? Notice that you frequently hold your breath. What relationship is there between your breath and the contractions of your stomach, and so on? When you have fully explored paired relationships, move on to concentrate on systems of interrelationships within the body.

STANDING AND RELAXING

So far you have been exploring the body at rest. In the following exercises, you will begin to move, and to begin concentrating on the world outside your own skin. These exercises are performed in a standing position, and you should devote some time to putting yourself at rest while erect.

Exercise 4: Hanging Yourself Up

As you stand, focus your attention on your skeleton. In the course of man's evolution, the skeleton has adapted itself to remain upright against the force of gravity with a minimum amount of effort. Imagine the bones within your body as a set of building blocks. Concentrating from the feet upward, stack the bones up in their proper order to achieve a self-supporting structure. Let the bones settle atop one another so that they remain in place with no muscular effort on your part. You will be standing in a relatively collapsed position, with your pelvic region and stomach thrust somewhat more forward than normal, your back and shoulders sagging more than is desirable. Practice this until you can stand with no muscular tensions whatsoever. If someone were to push you, you would unpile and crumple to the floor in pieces like a broken statue.

This posture is not particularly desirable on stage, since it is a very compact one and it is difficult for us to move freely from such a stable position. In order to achieve a highly flexible and responsive posture, repeat the exercise, but this time imagine that there are two wires attached to the floor beneath the heels of your feet, which run up to a junction at the center of your pelvis, and then extend upward in a single wire to the ceiling. Now imagine that your bones are hollow and that you are threading the bones one by one onto these wires. When the bones have all been threaded onto the wire, imagine that the wire is stretched upward. Feel yourself lifted toward the ceiling like a skeleton hanging from its spring. You are putting yourself into what the modern dancer calls "alignment." You must *not* have the sensation of pushing yourself up from the floor. You must instead feel yourself pulled up from above. It should be possible for you to remain elevated on the balls of your feet, even on the ball of one foot, for a good deal of time without unnecessary fatigue or wavering.

MOVING ON STAGE

Our purpose in standing erect in the above way is *not* to achieve a "correct" posture. For the actor there is no "correct" posture. This is simply the most balanced and effortless way to stand and still be ready to respond to the slightest stimulus. Placing yourself in alignment, try deciding upon a destination and then, with the slightest effort, "fall" toward that destination and "land" there. See how effortlessly you can initiate and terminate your movement.

An actor moving from one point to another on stage goes through much the same process as the musician playing a note on his instrument. The actor chooses his destination, just as the musician selects the pitch he intends to produce. Then, deep within him, the first energy of the movement is initiated, just as the musician's muscles produce breath, which causes the reed of his instrument to vibrate. So, too, the energy for your movement is initiated deep at the center of the body where the largest muscle systems intersect. This minute, initial vibration travels, expands, and is amplified by your body. Finally, the movement, like the sound of the instrument, erupts into the outside world in all its fullness. When the destination has been reached, the energy that initiated the entire process is expended and the movement ceases, just as the musician's note dies away when his breath is stopped. The exact quality of the movement, just as the timbre, amplitude, and color of the musical sound, is determined by the nature of the instrument (your body) and the way in which the instrument is played.

This is a way of saying that movements on stage must be clearly defined, that their shape must be self-contained—a beginning, a middle, and an end—and that they must be economical. Even if your character's mode of movement should be vague, purposeless, and confused, your *portrayal* of that kind of movement must be translated into clear and purposeful stage terms. You are not learning how to move "beautifully" or "correctly." You are learning how to control your movements fully in order to serve whatever purpose you have on stage in a forceful and economical way. If your character is ugly, awkward, or confused, you must present beautifully defined ugliness, forcefully purposeful awkwardness, and an absolute clarity of confusion.

Exercise 5: Punctuating Movement Part I

Practice moving from point to point around the stage, providing each movement with a clear beginning, middle, and end. Follow this pattern:

1. Select your destination and simultaneously
2. prepare to move by mobilizing the *entire* body,
3. then initiate the movement at the center of the body. Feel the pelvis, buttocks, small of the back, and abdominal muscles, and the massive muscles of the chest and back all involved from the outset of all your stage movements.
4. In the course of the movement, check for any muscular tensions providing obstacles between your desire to reach your destination and the free functioning of your entire body.
5. When reaching the destination, terminate the movement by "using up" the energy involved in it, and return to an aligned position. Purposefully *end* the movement. Think of the move as a sentence expressing one thought (the destination) and ending with a period.

SHAPING MOVEMENT FOR THE STAGE

Our relaxation and movement exercises are meant to eliminate *unnecessary* tensions which inhibit our responsiveness and freedom of movement; but tension itself, *properly used*, is an essential ingredient of theatrical performance. Tension, in this positive sense, is energy which has not yet been released in muscular activity and also energy which is balanced by an opposing force or obstacle. Such unreleased or counterbalanced energy is in a state of *suspense* (a term which describes something "held or prevented from proceeding").The suspense is over when the energy is expended in a completed action.

This principle applies equally to very small actions (like taking a single breath) and very large and complex actions (like the plot of a play). The moment when the action is "prevented from proceeding" or is just on the verge of proceeding is the moment of the greatest suspense. The stronger the held-back energy, the greater the suspense. The moment of suspense asks a question: how will the held-back energy release itself? What will happen?

Such a moment of suspense, when the outcome of an action hangs in the balance, is a *crisis* (a "turning point"). Most theatrical actions are shaped in this way: the action builds up energy and momentum until it reaches a crisis, it is held there in suspense, and then released. Aristotle even described the plots of most plays in this way. The period of rising energy he called the "ravelling," as it built up to the crisis, and the period of falling energy which followed the crisis he called the "unravelling" (our theatrical term *dénouement* is French for "unravelling").

The large pattern of action which forms the plot of a play is composed of a number of smaller units of actions, each of which has its own pattern of rising energy, crisis, and release. Each of these units of action is composed of yet smaller ones, and so on. Any large action is a collection of smaller actions linked in a purposeful way; usually the release of energy following one crisis forms the beginning of a rise toward the next crisis, and so on until the overall pattern has been fulfilled. If we can master the simplest of action-patterns and purposefully link them to other simple patterns, we can create limitlessly large and complex overall patterns (This will be discussed further in Lesson 12, *Play Structure and Action*).

Body movement is not the only way we express dramatic action on stage, but it is one of the most important and is our immediate concern here. From our heightened muscular participation in the pattern of actions can come a profound experience of our stage task.

The most basic body movement-pattern is that of a single breath. It clearly has a period of rising tension (inhaling), a crisis (a momentary holding of the breath), and a release (exhaling). Try taking a breath so as to heighten its dramatic potential: involve the entire body in the rise, crisis, and release pattern; start as "empty" as you can and rise to a high crisis; prolong the crisis, feeling the full strength of the held-back energy; and then release completely. A single breath can be an exciting theatrical event!

We heighten the "drama" of the breath by intensifying the pattern of its action in two ways. First we involve as many muscles as possible (and remember that a muscle can be at work without actually moving a great deal so that *all* our muscles can help support even the smallest action). This gives our bodies a chance to *resonate* the action fully, just as a musical instrument sounds richest when all of its parts join in vibrating the tone. Next we *extend the dynamic range* of the action by making the contractions smaller and the extensions larger, stretching the low and high points of the action farther apart.

Try taking another dramatic breath; when you have reached the prolonged crisis see what determines the "right" moment to let the breath out (besides simply not being able to hold it any longer). If you are responding to the shape of your whole action-pattern, the way in which you *exhale* will be determined by the way in which you have *inhaled.* In other words, each segment of an action-pattern should be proportioned to the others, in whatever way is appropriate in each case. This proportioning of the rise, crisis, and release of an action, and the way in which it is linked to other actions, is a principle factor of *rhythm.*

Rhythm denotes the patterned flow, the rise and fall, of energy and the temporal relationship between actions. It is the great unifying factor that gives cohesiveness to our work. Whatever the quality of the actions we perform, rhythm not only proportions them, it also integrates us with our actions. Rhythm is deeply rooted in our instinct, in our very existence, and will work for us if we freely involve and trust our muscles.

Exercise 5: Punctuating Movement Part II

Perform the following sequence of actions, attempting to realize fully the dramatic potential of each. Remember the two basic ways of intensifying action-patterns: *resonate* them by involving all your muscles in them, and *expand their dynamic range* by making the contractions small and tight, the expansions large and open. In each case identify the crisis; treat all that goes before as a preparation for the crisis and all which follows as a result. Prolong the crisis itself without breaking the overall rhythm of the action.

1. A single breath.
2. Ten breaths building to a scream.
3. A single step (in this and each following example continue exaggerated and audible breathing, inhaling during the rising action, holding the breath during the crisis, and exhaling during the release. You might like to try the actions with and without this parallel breathing to see how much the breath contributes to a sense of rhythm and to theatrical effectiveness).
4. Ten steps building to a leap.
5. Lowering your body into a chair (realize here how the pattern can be effectively reversed; a "falling" or contracting movement can express a rising segment of action, and *vice versa*).

6. Ten steps leading to sitting in a chair.
7. Finally, choose for yourself an action from life which is complete without being complex (for example, swatting a fly, getting a book off a shelf, changing a light bulb, or getting into a hot bath).

TRUSTING YOUR MUSCLES

The mind-body split we spoke of manifests itself in the actor who refuses to trust his own body, insisting on deciding and planning every move "in his head" before he lets his muscles do it. This sort of planning ahead, even if it is only a split second ahead, is a way of protecting ourselves from the threat of the unknown *here and now*. The right kind of preparation doesn't produce rigidity, and there are times when you must trust your body and be swept along by it; for the logic of the body, the way in which it operates because of the way in which it is put together, is the basis of all our expressive behavior.

Exercise 6: Action, Object, Emotion

Put yourself at rest and in alignment. Take a deep breath, hold it, then thrust your body and your breath outward at the same time, moving suddenly and *without plan*. Continue your random movements, allowing them to change until you discover some pantomimed object "touching" some part of your body. Don't let your mind decide what it is to be; let your muscles, in their random movement, suggest it to you. Keep asking your body, "Since you are moving like that, what might you be holding, standing upon, rubbing against" and so on. When you have discovered an object, continue to use it until an emotion grows in you. Again, *don't plan* the emotion, but let it be suggested to you by your activity. *How hard is it to avoid planning ahead? Can you see how much more "real" and imaginative the discoveries are that are truly made by the muscles?*

THE BODY AND THE THEATRE

The theatre is uniquely physiological in nature. In the theatre, the "instrument" that creates the experiences—the actor's total body—is identical with the "instrument" that receives the experience—the spectator's body. It is this biological identity between actor and spectator that makes the theatrical experience feelingful as well as comprehensible. This biological identity is expressed primarily in the nonverbal aspects of theatrical (as well as everyday) communication.

A psychologist recently found that the average adult in our culture spends only about twenty-five minutes a day in articulated speech. All the rest of the time he spends communicating with others (including those all-important pauses between words) is done by nonverbal means. It is also true that the eye is five times more efficient than the ear in terms of the amount and specificity of the information it can collect.

It is not surprising, then, that we live in a highly visual culture. How many times have you trusted your ears alone when dealing with life? You are in bed late at night when you hear a noise in the street below: are you satisfied to trust your ears to tell you what is happening? Or do you have to get up to collect the evidence of "your own eyes"?

All this indicates that the nonverbal aspects of our performance (the "dance" of our performance) is our primary tool. Furthermore, as we shall see later, the voice itself is only one of the modes of our total bodily expressiveness. For all these reasons, we begin our training program by concentrating on the body.

The picture of Willy Loman walking with bent back, shuffling across the opening scene of *Death of a Salesman*, communicates vividly an emotion, as well as surprisingly specific information about Willy's situation. So, in its own way, does the picture of Sheridan's Sir Anthony Absolute rushing wildly, powdered wig flying, before painted perspective flats. And so does the formal, precise striding of the Kabuki warrior as he employs the conventions of his theatre to reveal emotion and meaning. The highly artificialized movement required by some styles of drama is not an obstacle to the communication of the life contained in that drama. All drama, all styles communicate a sense of life. The genius of the actor is that he can communicate this life in the specific *form* in which it was conceived.

Therefore, the development of your physical tools is always geared to increasing your potential for the expression of life, yet at the same time, to increasing the fidelity with which you can communicate the form in which that life was originally conceived by the playwright. For this reason, do not limit yourself to the qualities of movement each of you experiences in everyday life, but study your bodies to develop the control necessary for the creation of whatever forms are required of you. The actor's study of his physical being is somewhat like learning the alphabet before beginning to read.

Before we move on, however, a cautionary word should be said about the essential nature and limitations of physical (or nonverbal) expressiveness in the theatre. If you have seen an expert mime perform, you know that a great deal of very specific information can be communicated nonverbally, but there are limitations as to the nature of the information that is best communicated in this way.

Generally speaking, nonverbal communication provides our sense of the intensity and depth of a feeling, while it is best left to words to communicate specific, factual information. We must also realize the importance of context in the specification of emotion, as Robert Breen explains:

> If emotion had to be judged solely from the external expressions, it would be difficult if not impossible for us to discriminate even such widely different emotions as joy and sorrow. It is not uncommon for people to cry in joy *and* sorrow. Discriminating subtler emotions would be even more difficult were it not for the fact that the psychological situation can be depended upon to identify the emotion. . . . Investigations of fear, rage, and pain showed no distinguishing features among the bodily changes which would discriminate these emotions. However, the situational responses of flight for fear, attack for rage, and aimless, uncoordinated movement for pain distinguished the emotions well enough.[7]

In other words, it is context (plot, the identification of character traits, and the audience's understanding of the situation in which the characters interact) that provides a *conceptual* understanding of the exact quality of emotion, but it is generally the nonverbal aspects of the performance (muscle tone, the breathing, inflections, and so on) that provide the *power* and *believability* of the emotion. Without this nonverbal foundation, our response to a play would be superficial or only intellectual.

The potentiality of nonverbal communication is great, but don't expect it to do a job for which it is not suited. A performance that is physically and emotionally powerful, but blurred in its outlines and lacking specificity of conception, is as faulty as an intellectually vivid but lifeless performance.

---

[7] Wallace A. Bacon and Robert S. Breen, *Literature as Experience* (New York: McGraw-Hill Book Company, 1959), p. 34.

Contacting Your Environment

In the last lesson you worked at contacting yourself, becoming more aware of the world inside your skin. It would be unfortunate, however, if your idea of awareness and organic wholeness were restricted to self alone.

Your organism functions within an environment, and you can have no meaningful sense of yourself without a heightened awareness of the world *outside* your skin. Furthermore, the behavior you will eventually portray on the stage is *expressive*, that is, behavior that reveals itself externally, in the ways your character copes with places, things, and other people. Therefore, it is essential that you begin to acknowledge your own organism's unavoidable participation in its environment.

The most basic and omnipresent aspect of your environment is the literal, physical *space* you occupy and which occupies you as well. The way in which you relate to this space is an important part of your expressive behavior, and developing an open and responsive relationship to life "outside" can start with an effort to contact your immediate space.

Exercise 7: Swimming in Space

Placing yourself in alignment, begin to move continuously (that is, without any specific destination) around your space. As you move, become acutely aware of any areas of tension within your body—in the buttocks, the small of the neck, the back of the calves, and so on. Concentrate on and agitate these areas until those tensions have evaporated.

When you are moving freely and effortlessly through space, concentrate your whole attention on the fluidity of your movement, becoming aware of the physical actuality of the space itself as you move through it. Boccioni's sculpture of a man walking (see Figure 1) shows a figure frozen in time, and behind it trail the aerodynamic patterns of the space through which it was moving. Become aware of the eddies and currents in space that you yourself are making. Uncover as much of your skin as possible and feel the resistance of the air as you move through it. Swing yourself wildly about, swimming in the ocean of the air.

Figure 1. The Body in Space (*Unique Forms of Continuity in Space*, by Umberto Boccioni, 1912.) Collection, The Museum of Modern Art, New York. Acquired through the Lillie P. Bliss Bequest.

Now concentrate your attention on the fact that the space is not only outside your skin, but comes inside your skin as well. Each breath takes in space. You are not only swimming through space, but *space is swimming through you.* The air through which you are moving is a fluid, and in every joint and cavity of your body there is also fluid. (One of the reasons that old persons move as they do is that the fluid that lubricates their joints has lost some of its viscosity. Try, as a side exercise, moving as if you had to overcome friction in each of your joints, as if you needed "oiling." You will find that this results in many movements characteristic of old age.)

Swim until you feel at one with your space, moving through it, it moving through you, overcoming its resistance, as well as being carried along by it. As you move, you carry along with you, in orbit as it were, a certain amount of space, which influences your momentum. An acute awareness of this will help you to move smoothly, so as not to violate the momentum of your "envelope" of space (unless of course, such violent movement is demanded by your role). As you walk and approach objects or other people in the room, sense the way in which you must change direction, pulling your space with you, pushing against space in a new direction in order to avoid collision.

Now become aware of the total space of the room, and all the objects, including yourself, which it contains. Concentrate fully on the way in which your movement influences the total shape of the room. See how every movement of your own and every movement of every other person in that space influences the total space.[8]

A STAGE IS A STAGE IS A STAGE

Everything that happens on stage . . . happens on a stage. The famine in ancient Thebes, the capture of Joan of Arc, a fight in a waterfront bar, God confronting mankind, mankind confronting nothingness; it all happens on *a stage*. The stage may be covered with painted canvas, lit with projections, or bare; it is still a stage. Actors can make a stage seem like any place, any time; but—it is, first of all, a stage. Until you have come to grips with the physical reality of the total stage, you have no foundation upon which to build further.

Stanislavski tells us that one of the first times he experienced full concentration (and therefore relaxation in the best sense) was in an exercise in which he counted the nails in the stage floorboards. The fact that the floor and its nails were *real* is important. Before you can go on to create the *illusion* of reality with vividness and commitment, you must establish contact with the *reality* of your working area, the stage. You must work in the here and now. The stage is the "here."

What is a stage? It is any area in which actors create for their audience the patterned experience called drama. The relationship of stage and audience is what spells the difference between one sort of stage and another. While your immediate concern may be the stage proper, that stage is only an artificially separated area within the larger theatre. It is this *total* theatrical space that is your true working area and the stage derives its meaning only from its relation to this total space.

During some periods of theatrical history the stage floor was sloped, or "raked" for a heightened illusion of perspective and for improved visibility of actors standing at the rear of the stage. For this reason we still speak of "*down*stage" as being toward the audience, and "*up*stage" as being away from the audience, since the stage floor was actually sloped in this way. Some modern productions have revived the raked stage.

---

[8] A complete program of excellent exercises is available in Viola Spolins, *Improvisation for the Theatre* (Evanston, Ill.: Northwestern University Press, 1965).

Lateral directions are determined by the right and left of an actor as he stands facing the audience. Thus "stage right" is the same as the audience's left. *Downstage right* means toward the audience and to the actor's right (see Figure 2). This basic system of giving directions is used on most types of stages.

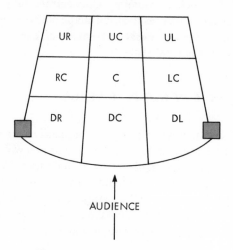

Figure 2. Traditional Directions on a Proscenium Stage.

Exercise 8: Saying Hello to the Stage

After learning the terminology for stage locations (Figure 2), move about on your stage announcing to the audience area your location, destination, and whatever you find on your travels. For example, "I am now standing upstage right and I am noticing a bump in the floor here and now I am crossing slowly down left, crossing center, where I see a floor marking from some past show, and now I am crawling in the down right area, seeing a different kind of flooring here, with old stage screw holes in it. . . ." Take your time and see how much of the stage area you can explore, concentrating fully on contacting the area and announcing your findings. Someone listening to a tape recording of your voice should be able to exactly recreate your movements and discoveries.

TYPES OF STAGES

Stages come in many sizes, shapes, and types. Anyone who has played "on the road," moving from one theatre to another, has had a vivid demonstration of the importance of an actor's responsiveness to his theatrical space. Never before has such a wide variety of stage types, each of which demands a somewhat different spatial attitude, confronted the actor. The basic types are three—*proscenium*, *thrust*, and *arena*—though there are many "in-between" variations (see Figure 3).

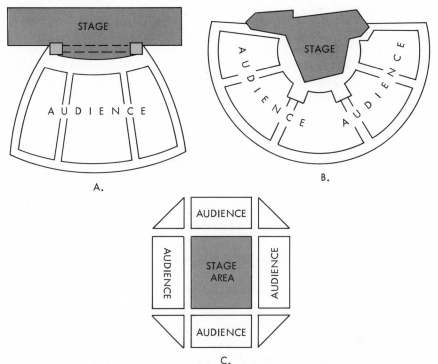

Figure 3. Types of Stages: A. Traditional Proscenium; B. Modern Thrust; C. Full-Round or "Arena."

PROSCENIUM. The traditional proscenium stage features an arch through which the action is viewed. It is thought that this "picture frame" developed as a way of establishing a frame of reference for settings painted in perspective (hence the word *pro-scenium*, meaning *in front of the scene*).

The actor on the proscenium stage must realize that his audience is limited to one side of his playing area, and he must accomodate himself to this fact. Standing behind the sofa during a crucial scene may not be a good idea, and neither is creeping continually upstage so that everybody else has to turn their backs on the audience in order to speak to you (hence the dreaded charge of "upstaging"). But the possibilities of good proscenium movement are greater than you might think and it is certainly *not* necessary to "cheat out" at all times as if you were more interested in speaking to the audience than to the person on stage with you (some actors are, of course). And don't underestimate how much acting you can do with your back. Strindberg said it was beyond his "wildest expectation" that he should ever see an actor's back during an important scene. So while you must accomodate your movement and positioning to the audience's location, you must also do so without destroying the internal logic of the stage space you inhabit. If the scene demands that you face and speak to the other actor, then *do it*—but ask your director to keep you where the audience can see you while you do it.

THRUST. Recently the thrust stage (so-called because it "thrusts" out into the midst of the audience) has come into great popularity. It features the same stage/audience relationship as the classical and Elizabethan theatres. It puts the actor into a close proximity with his audience but limits the use of scenery. For this reason, it is very much an "actor's" theatre and plays that, like the classics, utilize description and imagistic poetic devices seem more at home here than do realistic ones. The actor's movement can be described in the same way as on a proscenium stage, though here he is liberated from the audience's presence on only one side, and is freer to form three-dimensional patterns.

He has the added responsibility, however, of relating his movement to three sides and keeping hiself open to audience view, or at least distributing his presence equally to all sections of the house. This quickly ceases to be a problem when the actor realizes that the thrust provides a freedom to be used in an active, total way. The increased sense of audience participation inherent in the thrust stage inspires a warm and active sense of actor/audience contact, which makes such accomodation easy and natural.

ARENA. The arena and other types of full-round stages stand at the opposite extreme from proscenium stages. Here the actor enters through the audience area, either down the aisles or from "vomitoria" (openings cut into the sloped audience area; many thrust stages also have vomitoria for actor use). The problem of keeping open to all sections of the audience is more acute here than on a thrust stage not only because of the additional audience encirclement, but also because there is no "home base" to which the actor can relate. Nevertheless, a good actor's back can work wonders.

In thrust stages, the existence of a clear upstage area gives the actor some sense of direction; there is still an up and downstage. But in full arena, there is no upstage and downstage, or right and left, and the actor must remember that he always has his back to someone. Scenes requiring the actors to sit are especially hard here. But the full round does offer a sense of intimacy unlike any other type of stage, and such theatres are usually quite small. For this reason, audiences tend to expect a more detailed and subtle type of performance here.

In order to communicate directions in the full round, directors may either arbitrarily establish an up and downstage, or use some system of their own devising for numbering the stage areas. But most commonly they get along with such directions as "cross over by the telephone."

Most stages are variations of the three basic types discussed. Whatever stage you are on, your adaptations to the positioning of the audience, to the vocal demands of the shape and size of the house, and to the configuration of the stage are essential.

EXPLORING YOUR SPACE ON STAGE

The theatre is a physical space, and your treatment of that space is an important aspect of your performance. Your movement through the space of the stage, and your spatial relationship to the setting and other actors should express a meaning and logic of its own. This sculptural or *plastic* aspect of theatre is usually the main responsibility of the director and designer, but the actor's spatial sensitivity is as important for several reasons.

First, good stage movement depends upon extremely subtle adjustments, which the actors are often in the best position to make. Second, the spatially sensitive actor can understand and sometimes even assist his director much more than the sort of actor who seems unaware of where he is on stage. Finally, strong spatial awareness provides an actor with a basic channel of communication with his fellow actors. Your sense of your stage space is part of your over-all awareness of the here and now, and your ability to share this space with your fellow actors is part of your ability to contact them and help the *ensemble* to operate in the here and now as well.

The stage environment is filled with a multitude of inanimate objects, with sources of various sensations of sight, sound, touch, and smell, and with space itself. Before we begin to work with other people who share our stage environment, let us explore our physical relationship to the environment.

Group Exercise 1: Searching

I. All place yourselves at random throughout the stage space. Touch the physical environment with as much of your skin as you can: slither, crawl, roll. Move in a large circle from your position around as much of the theatre (audience area included) as you can cover, and back again. Do not deviate from your path no matter what objects you encounter (including other people), and fully explore all sensory qualities of each object and surface that you cross, all the time keeping as much physical contact with the theatre as possible.

II. With as much of your skin uncovered as possible, aggressively attempt to influence one another's space as you move continuously through the stage area. When driving on a highway, a passing car will suck another into its vacuum; become aware of this phenomenon as two persons pass one another. See what effect you can have on others by sweeping by them, pushing space at them, and so on, and what effect they can have on you.

III. All close your eyes and, keeping them closed, move very slowly throughout the stage space trying *not* to touch any physical object or surface or any person. Search with your skin, hearing, and smell for open space; crawl, stretch on tiptoe—whatever is necessary to find the most uninhabited space—but you must keep moving. See how, through practice, you can move with fewer and fewer collisions. Move more and more freely. *Any object or person touched must be identified by name before moving on.*

USING YOUR SPACE ON STAGE

Besides being your touchstones with reality, the physical objects that surround you on stage can also become active participants in your creation, if you can find ways to engage the environment in your performance and let it work for you. This exercise, and the one that follows, will help you to communicate with objects on stage.

Exercise 9: Stuff and Nonsense

Have everyone in the group bring an object of their choice to class, and litter the stage with these objects. Then take turns going onto the stage and repeating the "Saying Hello to the Stage" exercise (p. 22), handling all the objects, exploring each of them fully, while reporting your exploration to the group. Try to find characteristics of each object that no one else has noticed. As you explore each object, play a little scene with it, talking to it as if it were alive (though without changing it into anything else), introducing objects to each other. Try to invent a story in which all the objects are characters. Whoever invents the best story involving the most objects is the winner of the game.

TRANSFORMING YOUR SPACE ON STAGE

When you use your *real* stage environment to help you create an *imaginary* world, you try to find a way for each thing to help you. Many things that might seem distractions or obstacles to you at first can turn out to be valuable helpers if you find an imaginative way to use them. You needn't ignore any aspect of your environment (everything you ignore moves you one step further out of your here and now), nor must you have hallucinations and "really" see things that aren't there. Instead, you control your reactions to the things that are there, and make them fit your artistic purpose.

A child can look at a floating twig and see a great ocean liner, and he doesn't have to deny the existence of the twig to do so. He simply transforms his interpretation of what he is seeing. Yet when student actors are asked to visualize a scene, they invariably close their eyes, or stare off blankly into space, as if the things they might really see around them hindered their ability to pretend. They have lost the child's ability to contact and accept reality, and then *use* it to create an even more vivid illusion.

This ability is well worth regaining. The actor must continually relate to things on stage as if they were something else, but he must not lose touch with the reality of his situation in the process. Let us say that those hot spotlights are supposed to be a moonlit sky. Only a madman would fail to recognize the lights shining in his eyes, or the rows of people where a meadow ought to be. The actor accepts these sensations in all their reality, and then reacts to them *as if* they were sky and meadow. In this way, your responses can always be real, though the form in which they are expressed is artistically controlled.

PATTERNING YOUR SPACE ON STAGE

As you begin to contact and share your stage space, you will begin realizing what a potent tool space itself can be, when put to work properly. However, our movement through space, considered by itself, is abstract. Though it may have the same kind of abstract beauty as kinetic sculpture or modern dance, its effectiveness as stage movement depends on its relation to a meaningful context. Here are two exercises to help you examine both the abstract beauty of stage positioning and its potential meaningfulness as an expression of relationships between persons.

Group Exercise 2: Patterns I

As an entire group, put yourselves at rest and in alignment. Then all begin to move aimlessly, concentrating on the spatial pattern the group is forming within the room. As a basic pattern begins to emerge, join it until all members of the group are involved. As soon as everyone has joined in, stop all movement, concentrating on this emergent pattern. Then, on *individual* impulse, change your position so as to alter the basic pattern or your relationship to it. Continue doing this until the group has fallen into a new pattern, whereupon you all resume movement in the new pattern.

Then in motion, on individual impulse, break from the new pattern until it has distintegrated. The exercise may then be repeated. The group may possibly happen upon a group identity suggested by a discovered pattern, and such a discovery should be played out.

Figure 4. A "Patterns II" Exercise.

Exercise 10: Patterns II

With another member of the class, select a simple relationship (for example, mother/son, husband/wife, employer/employee, policeman/demonstrator, and so on) and begin, without further planning, to move in relationship to each other around the stage. Use no words. Do not begin with a specific situation or plot. Simply move until a pattern begins to emerge that seems to you both expressive of your relationship. Pursue this pattern until it becomes rigid; Let your individual qualities of movement be influenced as well. What has your movement taught you about your characters and their situation that you didn't know before? What did you communicate to your audience? How did your stage space and the location of your audience affect your movement? Did you use your space as a vehicle for your relationship?

Exercise 11: Patterns III

Using the relationship developed in Patterns II, one partner should select a simple message with a strong emotional potential (for example, "I want the money you owe me," or "You've just won a million dollars."), and without telling the other what it is, try to use your shared space and your movements in it to communicate the message. Use no words or signs of any sort; try to use *only* spatial means. When the partner begins to understand the message he uses space to try to communicate his reply (for example, "I don't have it," or "I don't believe you."). He can test his understanding of the message by testing the appropriateness of his reply. Again, attempt to use only *spatial* means. What patterns of movement emerged?

Good stage blocking should reflect basic character relationships as well as abstract spatial cause-and-effect. Though the director is primarily responsible for blocking, the actor's responsiveness to stage movement makes his blocking truly expressive and not merely "dead" motion. Even without a director's help, you should be able to utilize your stage environment to create expressive and spatially logical patterns, and as a vehicle to help you make contact with your fellow actors.

LESSON 3

Contacting Each Other

Other people are the most important part of our environment. The way they act upon, us, the way we act upon them, and the way in which we react to each other makes up the dynamic social process that largely shapes us and determines our mode of expression. This social process is of special importance to the actor, since the form of dramatic dialogue is a heightened and more or less ordered transformation of social interaction.

"Acting is reacting" is an old theatrical dictum, and a true one. Most of what you will ever do on stage will be in reaction to something else; your reaction will in turn serve as an action evoking its own reaction, and so the action moves. This means that the transference of energy from one character to another through the action-reaction/action-reaction chain is the main motive force moving the play forward. Supporting this chain must be the force of the real contact between the actors as teammates. Until they are truly acting and reacting upon each other as fellow workers, the interaction of the characters cannot be vivid and forceful. This communication within the acting ensemble is essential to good theatre.

THE ENSEMBLE

A stage production is successful only when it is the harmonious blending of the efforts of many artists. This makes acting a strictly *team* activity; thus, an important part of your discipline must be learning to work *with* other actors.

True, your individual skills will receive most of your attention and effort. You must develop an honesty and an intensity of response, and you must develop and expand the expressiveness of your voice and body until these things become no longer merely "technique." At the same time, you must develop your conceptual ability through the analysis and interpretation of scripts, discovering in them the materials provided by your playwright: rhythm, tones, emphasis, shape, direction, and function.

But you can do all this and still never participate in the truest artistry of the theatre, for that artistry lives only in the working of the creative ensemble. The playwright August Strindberg commented:

> No form of art is as dependent as the actor's. He cannot isolate his particular contribution, show it to someone and say, "This is mine." If he does not get the support of his fellow actors, his performance will lack resonance and depth. He will be held in check and lured into wrong inflections and wrong rhythms. He won't make a good impression no matter how hard he tries. Actors must rely on each other. Occasionally one sees an exceptionally egotistic individual who "upstages" a rival, obliterates him, in order that he and he alone can be seen.
>
> That is why good rapport among actors is imperative for the success of a play. I don't care whether you rank yourselves higher or lower than each other, or from side to side, or from inside out—as long as you do it together. [9]

When things have gone well, when the play, the actors, and the director have worked as an ensemble, and the audience has likewise given of itself, then there occurs one of those rare moments when true theatre lives, and all is justified. The actor achieves a sense of fulfillment greater than that of any other artist, because he does not experience it alone.

MAKING PHYSICAL CONTACT

Members of an athletic team must maintain strong communication with one another while performing the physical activity demanded by their sport, as must soldiers in combat, workmen in construction work, members of a symphony orchestra, and so on. In an endless variety of situations, we are thrown together in the physically dependent relationship of team effort, where the ability to work together is as important as individual skill.

This team relationship, grounded in the demands of physical cooperation, often promotes deeper and more pervasive relationships between individual team members. Psychologists are currently using group physical contact as a way of helping each individual to open himself to active and meaningful social relationships, which will in turn assist him in coping with his own problems.

Without undue interest in its therapeutic aspects, we can see that physical communication is essential to the actor. First, it promotes ensemble feeling. Second, it helps the individual actor to remain open and responsive, in the

---

[9] August Strindberg, "Notes to the Members of the Intimate Theatre (TDR Document)," trans. Everet Sprinchorn, *The Tulane Drama Review*, VI, no. 2 (November, 1961), p. 157. This material also copyrighted by *The Drama Review*, 1967.

here and now. Third, the movement of the play and the shaping of the theatrical experience depends upon the transference of energy in the action/reaction chain between actors. The two most important points are: first, that physical communication between actors must exist on all sensory levels, since the complete theatrical experience involves all the senses; and second, that it must be free of all inhibition.

For the first point: your ability to manipulate sensation is your "pallette," since all theatrical communication is at some point sensual. There is no ESP in the theatre; what is communicated, be it emotion or meaning, must be *palpable*, must be a sensation, before it can be experienced and interpreted by the audience.

For the second point: since you must act *totally*, making available not only all the senses but all parts of the body as well, and since it is often the actor's job to behave in a private manner in a public situation, you must overcome the social taboos that may restrict the completeness of your performance. This in no way means that you must abandon whatever moral standards in which you believe. It simply means that you must admit to yourself the highly physical nature of acting and behave accordingly.

Here are a series of group exercises used by dancers to help establish physical rapport.

Figure 5. A "Group Contact" Exercise.

Group Exercise 3: Making Contact[10]

1. *Blind Study.* All close eyes and move freely around the room, striving to vary movements (walking, crawling, rolling, turning, swinging, jumping, and so on) and constantly change. All must avoid all contact with others as they move. If contact takes place, the people who have touched must remain absolutely glued together at the point of contact, moving as a unit in a way determined by the strongest member. There is no limit to the size

---

[10] These exercises supplied by Carol Egan, Theatre Dance Program, Carnegie-Mellon University.

of the groups thus formed, and the eventual winner of this game would be the last single person not yet glued to someone else.

2. *Stealing Movements.* All start by doing individual free movement improvisations, trying to find new ways of moving. When someone sees another's movement that he likes, he "steals" it by moving in and mimicking it until the person from whom the movement is stolen abandons it. You must give up your movement shortly after it is stolen and find a new movement by stealing someone else's motif. All must be in constant change and constant awareness of others' movements.

3. *Orchestra.* A central figure acts as conductor before the group. All must follow his directions as he makes them rise, fall, turn, jump, move in circles, or do staccatto or legato movements, and so on. Anyone caught disobeying instructions must remain frozen in their disobedient posture; all should try to disobey without being caught.

4. *Tasks.* One person acts as director and calls out verbal commands to the group. He gives them tasks to perform as a group, as smaller groups, or as individuals. The tasks may involve pure movement, the use of props, vocalization, pantomime, and so on. Each continues performing the last task assigned to him until he is ordered to begin a new one. As random connections take place, join your tasks in such a way as to frustrate or assist each other.

SEEING AND HEARING EACH OTHER

As simple as they may seem, real seeing and real hearing are rare on the stage. As a way of avoiding the here and now, and maintaining selfish control of their individual performances, some actors only pretend to see and hear the other actors on stage. Actually, they are only superficially aware of their teammates. They are reacting instead to their imagined projection of what they would *like* the other actors to be doing, not to what is actually before them. Obviously, such reactions might *appear* correct to an audience, but the ensemble effort, and therefore the play as a whole, must inevitably suffer. Sometimes the selfish actor "gets away" with it, but only at the sacrifice of the fullest potential of his art.

Group Exercise 4: Mirror[11]

Divide the group into partnerships, assigning one partner the number "one," the other "two." At the beginning, partner "one" is the "real"

---

[11] The origin of the common "mirror" exercise seems to be a Stanislavski exercise here reported by I. Rapoport: "An example of such exercises is the so-called 'mirror' exercise. The two people doing the exercise stand opposite each other; one makes a movement, the other copies him exactly, as though in a mirror." I. Rappoort, "The Work of the

person, "two" is his mirror image. Trying to keep the partnership moving in unison, "one" makes slow "underwater" movements that "two" must mirror. The movements flow logically in a continuous stream. At the same time, he makes noises that reflect the movements and these must also be "mirrored." Notice how the movement and the noises are the vehicle for the communication; the bigger and more total and more continuous they are, the easier it is to stay together. Notice also that the communication must be a two-way street; "two" can keep up better when "one" is also responding to him.

At a signal, the roles are reversed *with no break in the action.* "Two" is now the leader, "one" is the follower. The roles are reversed a few more times until at last there is *no* leader. Without *either* "one" or "two" leading, but both following, the partnership continues to move and make noise together. At another signal, both close their eyes for a few moments while continuing to move. How well did you stay together?

Are there areas of your bodies that are not involved in the game? Did you begin to share emotions as well as noises and movements? Above all, were you really seeing and hearing each other?

Change partners often; try forming groups of three, four, and more persons, following the same process of allowing each to lead, then moving without a leader.

PHYSICAL REALITY AND
CREATED ILLUSION

So far we have been stressing the need to contact our physical reality in space and time; how will this help us in creating the "illusion" of our role? How does our reality relate to our creation? In answering this question, we must beware of the vagueness of terms like "illusion" and "reality." It is difficult to say where illusion begins and reality leaves off. Theatre, at its best, transcends the narrow definition of these terms. It is a place where illusion and reality mix inseparably.

The trouble with the idea of "illusion" in theatre, as in other arts, is that the "illusion" of art is often more "real" than "reality." Tennessee Williams puts it beautifully when his character Tom in *The Glass Menagerie* says to the audience:

> I am the opposite of a stage magician. He gives you illusion that has the appearance of truth. I give you truth in the pleasant disguise of illusion.

Let us abandon the distinction between reality and illusion, and instead speak

Actor," *Acting: a Handbook of the Stanislavski Method,* ed. Toby Cole, (New York: Crown Publishers, Inc., 1955), p. 38. Used by permission.

of various *levels* or kinds of reality that coexist within the theatre, each of which contacts the audience in its own way and for its own purpose, but also interacts with the other realities.

Instead of "illusion," we will use the term "aesthetic reality." This phrase implies that the product of the performance, the thing that used to be called "illusion," is itself real. If you think back to successful performances you have seen, you will remember characters and places created by the actors and designers as having a reality *of their own*, not necessarily "better" or "worse" than the reality of the actors and the scenery, which you also remember, but existing simultaneously in a different way.

We will call the "reality" of the actors and the scenery the "social reality," referring to the identity between actors and audience members as human beings existing *within the same social sphere*. The theatre itself has a physical existence, a social reality, as a place within which aesthetic reality is created and communicated. The *aesthetic reality*, then, refers primarily to the audience's relation with the *character* and his world, while the *social reality* refers primarily to the audience's relation to the *actor* and the theatre.

THE INTERRELATIONSHIP OF THE SOCIAL AND THE AESTHETIC

Having substituted our idea of levels of reality for the usual distinction between illusion and reality, we see that the various levels are simultaneous aspects of a unified experience. The relationship between these levels, moreover, is constantly shifting and is a source of theatrical dynamism.

The social reality binds you and your audience together. On a basic level, you accept the presence of your audience as real people, and are sensitive to their responses to your performance. Likewise, they accept you as a real human being and are sensitive to you as a performer. We are sometimes tempted to ignore this social reality, or even to consider it antithetical to the aesthetic reality. Some overly cautious directors are tempted to block fights, for example, as extremely polite bouts, with the actors clearly in no danger of doing each other actual harm. These directors argue that "negative empathy" will arise if the audience becomes too concerned about the actor's physical well-being, and this awareness of the *actor* will supposedly destroy the "illusion" of the *character*. Their aim is to make the audience forget that it is in a theatre; they suppress the social reality entirely, in favor of the aesthetic reality.

Much modern theatre, however, assumes that there is no such incompatibility between social and aesthetic realities. The plays of Bertolt Brecht, for example, are designed to remind the audience continually that they are really in a theatre, watching actors performing. Playwrights like Tennessee Williams,

Arthur Miller, Thornton Wilder, Samuel Beckett, Eugene Ionesco, Robert Bolt, Jean-Claude van Itallie, and many others, manipulate, each in his own way, the social reality as an overt and purposeful element of the total theatrical experience. This is in some measure a return to the strong flavor of the classical theatre and, indeed, many of the devices of the contemporary theatre (narrators and choruses, direct address, masks, episodic structure, and so on) are familiar classical techniques relating directly to the social reality of actors and the theatre.

THE ACTOR AND SOCIAL REALITY

One of the very first problems the young actor must solve is how to come to an honest acceptance of the social realities of the theatrical situation. Until you have done this, you are not really "there" on stage. You are wasting valuable energy in ignoring the reality of your situation, rather than in using it in the creation of your performance. The actor who is not really "there" makes it very difficult for the audience to become engaged in his performance. The aesthetic reality we create on stage must be built upon an acceptance and utilization of the social reality of our presence on stage. The more *actual* we can make our contact with ourselves and with our real environment, the stronger our aesthetic reality can be. Though the aesthetic reality is a *transformation* of the social reality for artistic purposes, it nevertheless depends upon it as its only source of power and vitality.

Exercise 12: Defining Reality

Think back to a performance you have seen recently. Try to list all the sensations you, as an audience member, had in the first ten minutes.

1. Which sensations were related to the social reality?
2. Which related to the aesthetic reality?
3. Which related to both?
4. How did each of your sensations contribute to your experience of the play? Where some helpful and others harmful? Can you really distinguish between levels of reality at those moments when the play is working well?

ACTOR AND AUDIENCE

An attitude that is the hallmark of much recent theatre (and of contemporary arts in general) is that there is no *essential* difference between the artist (actor) and the spectator (audience). The actor watches his own performance at the same time that he is involved in creating it, and this makes him a special sort of audience member; the audience members participate in the performance at the same time that they watch it, and this makes them actors of a special kind.

This is a return to the communal experience of the Classic theatre, in which the active participation of the audience is necessary for the complete realization of the drama. The aim is to make the social reality and the aesthetic reality combine so thoroughly that the result is a new kind of experience, which transcends both the social relationship of audience and actor and the aesthetic relationship of audience and character by combining them into a unique *theatrical* experience.

It is important, therefore, to accept the audience's presence. If you ignore your social relationship to the audience, if you pretend that there really isn't anyone out there watching you, you cut yourself off from vital avenues of communication, which can be utilized for the benefit of your creation, a creation in which the audience must participate. The play must not remain trapped either on the stage or in the mind's eye of the audience, but must be free to exist within the total theatrical environment, free to receive the contributions to its life of both audience and actor.

Of course, this is only a general principle. Each play requires a different emphasis *within this general idea*. The stage life of some plays, especially naturalistic ones, is relatively self-contained and partially independent of the audience's response. Other plays, like Brecht's, require the audience's full participation. Most plays adopt a *variable* position. There are a good many different kinds of theatre, each kind requiring its own particular mode of communication between stage and audience. An important part of the actor's and director's job is to discover and establish the particular kind of stage/audience relationship that each play demands. We should, therefore, keep in mind that our relationship with our audience is in part an expression of the play's style and the director's production concept, and should not be limited by the narrowness of one fixed attitude toward the theatrical environment.

Exercise 13: Audience/Actor

Using the same list of sensations from the last exercise, see how many of your audience sensations were shared by the actors. Then, imagining yourself one of the actors, see how many of your sensations would have been shared by the audience. Is there any one kind of sensation that actors never share with audiences, and vice versa?

A word of caution is in order. Except in those plays in which the audience's presence becomes an overt element of the play's structure through such devices as direct address, dialogue with audience members, actors mingling with the audience, and so on, the audience's reaction is not the immediate *purpose* of our performance. Even in such plays, the audience is treated artistically as a "character" in the play. Therefore, our immediate task on stage is always to fulfill our character's dramatic objective, not to create a response in our audience. Certainly our audience's response is important, and we shape our way of fulfilling dramatic objectives with an eye toward audience response. But when we are actually performing, our immediate concentration is on *what* we are doing, not on the audience's response to it.

It will be best to think of the audience's presence as *part of your stage environment*. To be in touch with your total environment, you must also be in touch with the audience, just as you are in touch with your fellow actors. You, your fellow actors, and your audience are all teammates working *together* to create the drama. You do not "play for the sake of" your audience, any more than you "play for the sake of" your fellow actors. You are *all* working toward the same goal, which is the expression of the intrinsic vitality of the drama.

Emotion and
the Body

What is *emotion*? The root meaning of the word is *an outward movement*. For us, it is any activity that is an expression of the immediate condition of our organism and is directed toward the world outside our skins. This doesn't mean that emotional expression is always meant to be communicative. The expression of an emotion is part and parcel of the emotion itself. Most forms of emotional expression are symbolic activities, which provide some sense of satisfaction either as substitutes for real success, or as extensions of real success that heighten our pleasure. In this way, emotions are a "safety valve," which provides a release of tensions (pleasant or unpleasant). Our organisms tend to seek equilibrium and a reduction of tensions, so emotions are one of our basic adaptive mechanisms.

Further, emotional expression helps us to *realize* our own condition, to objectify and clarify it *for ourselves*. By forming an emotional reaction to something, we "get it off our chests" and crystallize its meaning for us. For example, many people are impatient with much modern theatre because they don't know "if it's supposed to be funny or what." They don't know how to cope with it until they decide what emotional response is appropriate, since they are accustomed to their emotional response providing a frame of reference for most experiences. Another example is when we ask, "Are you putting me on?" If the answer is yes, we may laugh; if it is no, we may be angry. In either case, the formation of an emotion formalizes our response, and until the emotion is formed, we may suspend our judgment of a situation.

Emotion, therefore, serves the needs of the individual. Though much of our emotional expression is aimed at communicating our feelings to other people, emotions themselves are part of our very being. This is also true of a character in a play. Though the emotions of a dramatic character are designed to serve a certain purpose in his play, they, too, must be made part and parcel of our portrayal of that character, and not left simply as sensations we communicate to our audience.

EMOTION IN THE THEATRE

Emotion is a dangerous commodity in the theatre. The qualities that distinguish an *effective* emotion (one which supports, extends, and helps communicate the play's meaning) from an *ineffective* one (one that obscures meaning or intrudes on the play's progress) are very slight. And yet no aspect of performance is harder to regulate, especially for the young actor who is eager to create the great emotional "experience."

Young actors are often tempted to admire the powerful emotional impact of the actor who totally loses control of himself. But we must remember that the sheer experience of emotion for its own sake is not our true purpose. An actor may feel selfishly successful if he makes his audience weep, but he has failed if his audience's weeping does not lead to a fuller, more vivid, more honest understanding of the play as a whole. The great actor aspires to use his emotional technique to realize fully the truth of his character, in terms of the play in which that character appears. In other words, the ultimate test of a performance is not simply its emotional power, but the completeness with which it contributes to the whole play as a work of art. For the actor, emotion is a means to this end, never an end in itself.

The proper theatrical purpose of emotion is to make the action of the play and its meaning more immediate for the audience, to help them experience the character's situation and activity more vividly. Each play uses emotion in a different way. Some appeal to sentiment, others try to appeal to more profound passions, and some even attempt to be "*un*emotional" in order to focus their appeal on our reason. But in all plays, emotion on the part of the characters, whatever response is expected from the audience, helps to move and vivify the action.

THE GENESIS OF EMOTION: THE JAMES-LANGE THEORY

Near the turn of the century, two psychologists, Fritz Lange and William James, developed a theory of emotion of special interest to the actor (Stanislavski was familiar with it), because of its physical orientation.

This theory holds that emotion is identical with its muscular symptoms. What we call "grief" is not a description of a "mental" state, but a description of convulsive sobbing, tears, shortness of breath, and erratic body tempo. Our emotion *is* its bodily manifestation; our *concept* of the emotion is our recognition of our bodily condition.

Let's say you are stepping off a curb when, out of the corner of your eye, you see a car rushing toward you. Of course you leap back out of danger. You are afraid, but you did not jump *because* you were afraid. If you had to wait for the emotional response to motivate your action, you would have been too late. You reacted *automatically* (or viscerally) to the signal of danger. It was a direct motor response, which bypassed conceptual thinking. Then, with your heart pounding, adrenalin flowing, your breath short, you conceptualized your condition and called it "fear."

This is also called the "fright-flight" theory: you do not run because you are afraid; you become afraid because you are running. Not all emotions in life are generated in this way, but all emotions *do* involve a bodily symptom. Without some bodily symptom, there is no emotion. When we suppress the normal symptoms of an emotion, it will redirect itself and reappear in an unusual form. Peter, in *The Zoo Story*, for example, inhibits the direct outpouring of his feelings, until they find their own release in his uncontrollable, hysterical laughter.

This can explain how we communicate the physical vividness of an emotion to an audience through the audience's imitation of striking and carefully constructed physical images. The communication begins as simple physical imitation; then, because the audience's muscles are responding similarly to those of the actor, similar feelings are inspired in them. In this way, the audience shares the character's emotion, rather than simply observing it. If the character weeps, the audience feels a "sympathetic" (actually "imitative") lump in its throat. As Willy Loman shuffles across the stage, back bowed, the audience participates physically in his exhaustion and dejection.

THE ACTOR AND THE JAMES-LANGE THEORY

We can adapt this theory to the needs of the actor by proposing that if we adopt the external or physical symptoms of an emotion, the internal fullness of that emotion will grow within us (assuming that we have developed strong responsiveness to our own physical state and have overcome the many inhibitions that "control" our emotions). This is a useful attitude for the actor since his script provides him with a wealth of external details to be utilized in achieving an internalization of the life of the character. A play script contains not only specified actions, but a whole range of implied externals embodied in its rhythms, emphases, meanings, images, and over-all structure. By participating physically in these externals, we imitate the character. By understanding and respecting the character's dramatic function and style, we can help ourselves develop identification with him. Finally, by mastery of the techniques of stage performance, we can communicate this fully expressed characterization to our audience.

William Ball, of the American Conservatory Theatre, has been developing training techniques based upon the dictum, "Do the act and the feeling will follow." There are three important qualifications to be made, however. First, what *is* the action that generates emotion? Most of the overt emotional acts we might think of (for example, hitting the table when angry) are actually safety-valve actions, which erupt when tension has reached a certain level. They are not actions that will generate emotion so much as they are the *results* of emotional tension. One can pound the table for hours and generate little more than a sore hand; it is the activity, the tension, that would *cause* us to pound the table which we must emulate if we wish to generate rage.

Second, we must perform the *proper* activity in order to generate the appropriate feeling. Playwrights generally answer this qualification for us by providing carefully designed externals, as discussed above.

Finally, in order to be responsive to our own actions, we must be "in touch" with ourselves. If we have not contacted ourselves, then the actions we perform will have no effect upon us. Our aim in "doing the act" and letting the "feeling follow" is to allow the internalization of our action to become *self-generating*. Our basic actions lead us in turn to fuller actions, which become the true extensions of the actions provided by the play, in the fullness of our rejuvenation of the text.

We must also remember that while the actor's emotional *energy* is one of his basic tools, the *form* any emotional expression takes on stage must be consistent with the demands of the play's style. We study emotional expression in real life in order to discover the *principles* that underlie expressive behavior, not because emotion on stage is always expressed in the way it might be in everyday life. A character of Shakespeare's and an O'Neill character might need to express similar emotions, and the actor would have to supply the same degree of emotional *energy* in order to vitalize the character's feelings, but probably the form in which the emotion would be expressed would be different in each case.

Our skill in analysing and understanding our text and its style will provide our understanding of the required form, but until we have developed these skills (in Part II), you can use this simple exercise as a way of testing your own ability to work from the externals of emotional expression toward a self-generating internalization. It also tests your ability to retain the energy of that emotion while transforming it into a new style of expression.

Exercise 14: Emotion Adoption

From your own experience or, better, from real life observation, reconstruct in minute detail the physical characteristics of someone's intense emotion. Consider each area of the body and its behavior. Do not neglect the breath and the general motor rhythm and tone. Do not think about the *reason* for the emotion or even the exact quality of the emotion in its

completeness. Concentrate instead on the simple, mechanical manifesta-
tions of this emotion in the body. Think of the physical traits of the emotion as parts of a costume you are putting on. Beginning at the bottom of
your body and moving upwards, adopt the behavior you have analyzed.
Throw yourself fully into it. See if the proper emotional state begins to
grow within you. Which aspects of your behavior seem to contribute most
to the development of this feeling? Can you find vestiges of animal activity
in each aspect of the behavior? Here is an example:

> "I am curling my toes against the floor so as to have a firm footing in
> case I have to spring either in attack or retreat. I am shifting my body
> weight forward on the balls of the feet so as to be as mobile as possible.
> My legs are bending so that my body can spring. This causes great tension
> in my calves and thighs. This bent posture is also a good defense, since
> several vulnerable areas of my body (my genitals, my abdomen, my neck,
> my eyes) are protected. I have drawn my arms in so as to protect the center
> of my body, but at the same time, my hands are upraised for defense.
> My fingers are curled; this is perhaps a vestige of a time when man had
> claws. My shoulders have hunched forward so as to protect my neck. My
> jaw is very tense and my lower jaw is thrusting out. It is as if I still had
> fangs and was preparing to tear at my opponent's throat. My brow has
> sunk down to protect my eyes, which have narrowed to thin slits. This
> generally defensive posture has made me breathe in a restricted manner,
> because my diaphragm can no longer travel its full extent. But because of
> the increased need to oxygenate my muscles, I compensate by breathing
> more rapidly. The general tension in my body is growing; I feel a cold
> sweat breaking out in the palms of my hands and on my forehead. My
> breath is coming erratically now and I am beginning to make guttural
> noises. If I attempt to speak, I find that my tone is the tone of an extreme-
> ly angry person. In fact, I feel rage beginning to swell up in me. . . ."

Continue the development of this sensation by thrusting yourself more
and more intensely into your physical situation. Avoid thinking about
anything but your own body. As the emotional state grows, let it wash over
you and extend itself to its own necessary conclusion. In this case you may
perhaps finally plunge forward, slam your fist on a table, or let out a bellow
of rage. A point will come when your suppressed tensions must result in
overt reaction. The "emotional outburst" is an "overflow" or "safety
valve" action.

In this exercise, you may have found yourself discovering a basic sort of
characterization arising from your involvement in an active emotional state.
Since you took your observation of the emotion from someone else, does the
realization that you now have about this emotion seem appropriate to your
model? What new information does it give you? If it does not seem appropriate, what might have gone wrong? Which aspects of your behavior

influenced the development of the emotion most? Try doing this exercise in front of the class and compare their impression of your behavior with what you are feeling and with your original model. Now try the next exercise.

Exercise 15: Emotion Adoption in a New Form

Attempt to recreate for yourself the emotion adopted in the previous exercise, but this time try to experience it as it would be expressed by a Greek tragic hero (if it is unpleasant) or a *commedia dell'arte* character (if it is pleasant). Examine *each detail* that you observed in real life, and evaluate it in terms of its appropriateness for this new form. Should it be kept, or is it too unessential for the economy demanded by stylized forms? If it is kept, how must it be transformed? What is essential and useful in this form; what isn't? Can you experience the energy of the emotion as strongly in this new form? Is the quality of the experience different?

BREATH AND EMOTION

Most actors agree that the most effective tool we have for the communication and expression of emotion is the breath. The next time you see a performance try to become aware of the impact that an actor's breathing can have on the audience. One negative example would be the actor who breathes with great tension, who has not learned to relax. His voice comes out in strained fashion and the muscular tensions are rapidly communicated to the audience, who respond with a wave of coughing and restlessness. They have "caught" his tension. On the other hand, effortless breathing can help to quell nervousness. When experiencing stage fright, taking a deep breath will help to relax you.

It is perfectly appropriate that the breath should be at the root of most of our emotional states. The word *psychology* itself means "study of the soul," and the word for soul, *psyche*, originally meant "vital breath." Common superstition is that the expiring breath of a dying man is his soul leaving his body.

Besides the breath's obvious importance for life, there is another way of describing its importance in the expression of emotion. As we have said, emotion usually is the result of our attempt to adapt to the outside world. The ways in which we most directly contact the outside world are therefore the primary means of emotional expression. Remember the space exercise in which you became aware of space moving through your body? It is through the breath that we literally bring the outside world into our bodies and then expel it again, and the way we feel about that outside world will be expressed by the way in which we breathe it in and breathe it out. Take, for example, a sudden and unexpected danger. It would seem that the physiological necessity of coping with whatever is threatening us would make us breathe rapidly in order to oxygenate our muscles, and indeed, when the initial shock has worn off, our fear is expressed by rapid and shallow panting. But our initial reaction at the time of the first shock is just the opposite: we take a sudden breath and quickly shut the mouth, and then *hold* our breath for a period of time. It is as if we are saying to the outside world, "You threaten me; you can't come in; I'm closing the door to you." This is what a psychologist might call "playing dead inside our skins."

Exercise 16: Breath and Emotion

Place yourself at rest in a comfortable position. Concentrate on your breath: its frequencies, its rhythm, its depth. Begin to manipulate the breath as if you were improvising on a musical instrument. Concentrate on the sounds and feel of the breath for its own sake; do not think of "emotions" or "experiences." Concentrate only on the breath *per se*. You will become aware of shifting and momentary moods, which will play across your consciousness as a result of your changing breath pattern.

At this level, any feelings that might be motivated by your breath manipulation would be vague and undifferentiated, and can best be called "moods." There is good reason to view the emotional development of the human being, as well as the process by which individual emotional experiences grow, as beginning in a state of simple unspecified turbulence. In this undifferentiated form, emotion is simply increased energy and excitement in response to a stimulus. It is only as the emotion develops that it begins to take on unique characteristics of its own. As we suggested in the last lesson, there is a basic level of theatrical communication, which provides the sense of emotional intensity that must then be further specified and clarified by our understanding of character and situation. Just so, in this exercise, we begin to sense the germinal state of emotion as an unspecified increase in excitement, which nonetheless contains the seed of further specification. This undifferentiated excitement may be called "anxiety."

The particular value for the actor in tracing the development of emotion is that it enables him to regulate directly the sights and sounds he produces for his audience. He need not depend on some mental image to motivate his emotional expressiveness; he can move directly and actively into the emotional realm. Beginning with the breath has the particular advantage of providing a direct route to three highly expressive aspects of performance: our general muscle tone and rhythms, facial expression, and the quality of our speech. Continue the exercise now to explore these areas.

Exercise 17: Emotion and Voice

Continue your concentration upon a manipulation of your breath. Become aware of the effect that various breath rhythms have upon the general muscle tone of the body. Explore pleasant and unpleasant kinds of breath patterns. In breath that is short, irregular, and rapid, you will find that an unpleasant sense of anxiety may be produced. See how this anxiousness affects the general muscle tone and rhythm of your body. Try moving in this state, and see how the rhythms of your muscular functions are affected. What expressive qualities result?

Now return to a comfortable position. Continue breath manipulation. Concentrate on your facial expression. Do not attempt to manipulate it, simply become aware of it. You will be surprised at the rapidity of its changes and how directly the breath influences it. Begin to make sounds. The sounds may form themselves into articulated speech, but avoid making up speeches. Your breath manipulation will have an immediate effect upon the loudness and quality of your speech, and expressive inflections will arise automatically.

We see that the voice is profoundly influenced by the muscular conditions of emotion. Playwrights, knowing this, will have provided rhythms, tones, and inflections useful to you in recreation of the character's emotion. In fact, as we will learn later, it may be possible to learn a great deal about the emotional quality intended by the playwright by studying these aspects of his text.

BREATH AND EMOTIONAL COMMUNICATION

Just as we can increase our awareness of the expressiveness of our own breath, we can increase sensitivity to the breath of others.

Exercise 18: Breath Scene

With a partner, select a scene from a play, preferably one involving an intense emotional interchange, or one in which the emotional pattern of the two characters is sharply different. Perform the scene, concentrating on the shape of the emotions communicated between the characters, using only breath and nonverbal noises. Do not pantomime or "charade" the content of the scene; your objective is to communicate intensely with each other through breath and breath noises alone. Move as actively as possible. *Do not be limited to a realistic approach to the scene.* As you try this exercise, many things may occur to you; explore them freely. You may find yourself behaving as a sort of animal or machine; whatever occurs to you, do whatever necessary to explore the communicative potential and inherent meaning of your breath and the noises of your voice for their own sake.

You will probably find that meaningful communication is possible only when you both move as freely and vigorously as possible. The breath and noises that you produce involve an enormous number of muscles, and only when the entire body is actively participating in their production can you hope to communicate effectively. Do not think about the emotions as concepts or even memories, but focus on your breath communication.

ACTION AND EMOTION

We have been talking about the breath as a starting point for emotion but there are other starting points as well. The breath is produced and controlled by a complex system of muscles, which influences all parts of our body. These same, and other, muscles are used in all large actions. Here is an exercise that examines the evocation of emotion by physical actions not necessarily related to breath.

Exercise 19: Action to Emotion

Without thinking about it in advance, begin to move violently in some manner. Continue this movement and concentrate upon it until an emotional attitude begins to grow spontaneously from it. Allow the emotion to develop until it specifies itself clearly. It may begin to suggest to you a situational context. Your thoughts might be something like, "I am jumping up and down. I am beginning to breathe very hard. When I make a noise, my pitch is very high and my phrases short. I sound like a little girl. I am very happy and excited. I am about to be given a present." And so on. See how far you must go to complete the process you have set in motion. In this example, you might finish with a squeal of delight and a grasping and hugging movement.

THE CONTINUITY OF EMOTION

So far we have been discussing emotions as if they had a beginning and ending. This is a common misconception, which we should clarify.

Emotion is not *periodic*, it is *continuous*. It arises from the success or failure of our attempts to adapt to the world, and may be considered as our evaluation of the effectiveness of our adaptations. As such, it is continuous and immediate. It is vital to our well-being "for it not only furnishes the basis of awareness of what is important, but it also energizes appropriate action, or, if this is not at once available, it energizes and directs the search for it."[12] Emotion is an unending process, since we are continually evaluating our relationships with the outside world.

Actors often make the mistake of regarding emotions as periodic outbursts in their characters, which flare up and then disappear, the character progressing from one emotion to another. But there are two aspects of our character's emotional make-up; his *dominant* mood, which is continuous, and his *phasic* mood, which is changeable. Early in your development as an actor, you will successfully achieve striking moments of emotional expression. Such momentary emotions are only phases through which the character passes. Beneath these changing emotional phases is a continuity of expression and feeling, which is much more subtle and difficult to achieve. The momentary or "phasic" emotion is easier to achieve because it is intense and spectacular, but the test of the great performance is the communication of the dominant and continual existence of the character that underlies and gives meaning to phasic emotions.

The emotional life of our character, therefore, does not "begin" and "end," but rather is continuous, with phasic emotions swelling up to the surface at certain times. The potential for these phasic emotions, however, is a permanent aspect of the dominant mood. In *The Zoo Story*, Jerry's suicide must be an integral part of his personality. At the beginning of the play, it is a submerged element of his personality; we must not feel his potential for suicide too soon. But when, at the end of the play, it swells up, then we must realize that it has been there all along. Think of a character's emotional make-up as a complex musical chord containing many notes. As a whole, the chord has a unified sound into which each individual note is submerged. But the dynamic vitality of the character's changing life is achieved by allowing first one note, then another, to swell up until it can be picked out for its own sake. Though we may recognize it for its own sake at such moments, we also realize for the first time that it has been there all along.

EMOTION AND EXTERNAL OBJECTS

We see that emotion must, in its fullest intensity, exist within a situational context. Most of the emotions of which we are capable exist deep with-

---

12 Perls, Hefferline, and Goodman, *Gestalt Therapy*, p. 95.

in us in a dormant state and are suddenly called forth by the demands of our situation.

Exercise 20: Emotion Potentials

As a member of a small group, repeat Exercise 19, using some emotion from your actual experience. Insert it into some imagined context taken from the *immediate present*. For example, if you begin with "frustrated anger," you might imagine that one of the members of your group has just insulted you. If you choose "grief," you might imagine that one of your group has died. Observe each other perform this exercise, and discuss in the group how each person's potential for the emotion he performed is expressed in his everyday behavior. For example, we might say to the person who has expressed anger, "Your anger is of a very actively physical kind. The way you shook your fist and pounded the table reminds me of the way in which you throw yourself into a chair when you come into the room or the way in which you write so vigorously when you are taking notes, or the way in which you tend to tear at your food during lunch," and so on.

In its fullest expression, emotion needs an external object toward which it is directed. If there is no external object immediately at hand, we will find a substitute. Often we will "take out" our emotion on someone who had nothing to do with the original feeling. Or, we will perform some *symbolic* action (like punching our own hand) to provide at least a symbolic external object. This is a basic problem the actor must solve when expressing emotion: what external objects or persons are available toward which he can direct the emotion? Usually you will find that a skillful playwright will have provided such an object, even though it may be only a symbolic one. In *The Zoo Story*, Peter's main function as a character is to serve as such an object, toward which Jerry directs his general *malaise*.

By seeing what the external object of emotion may be in each scene, you will discover much about the quality of the emotion and its expression. In *King Lear*, for example, Lear begins by railing against individuals: Kent, Cordelia, his daughters. During his madness, he provides external objects for his emotion by imagining that he sees a convict, a justice, a grand lady, even Goneril and Regan themselves. But later on, his feelings have much more symbolic, generalized objects, such as the gods themselves. This reveals to us the way in which Lear's emotion grows beyond the limits of his immediate situation to an almost existential concern for all mankind.

The actor's problem is to localize the emotional object at each moment and make real contact with it. Here is an exercise for moving the focus of our emotion out of ourselves and into the reality around us.

Exercise 21: Emotional Objects

With a partner, choose a short scene from a play involving strong emotions. Try the scene several times, each time using different external objects for the emotion.

1. Use an irrelevant object: a fireplug, or chair, and so on.
2. Use a symbolic object: translate any emotional activity (like hitting the other person) into strictly symbolic activity (like tearing pieces of paper).
3. Use a verbal object: translate the emotion into words, or create an imagined object for the emotion in words (Jerry does this continually in *The Zoo Story*, using his various "stories" as vehicles for the expression of underlying emotion.)
4. Use a direct object: contact each other physically. Analyze your performances. Was the most direct one necessarily the most interesting, or was more revealed when direct action was inhibited and the emotion channeled through an indirect object instead?

Now analyze the scene and see what objects have been provided by the playwright. What does this tell you about the scene and the characters?

LESSON 5

Physical Gesture

Emotion, though we may be acutely aware of it as an interior excitation, cannot be communicated until it has resulted in some external sign observable to others. Broadly speaking, such an external sign may be called a *gesture*. When we commonly speak of "gestures," we usually refer only to physical movements, but here we refer to the whole range of external emotional signs. Gestures can be both nonvocal and vocal, for the noises we produce apart from articulated speech are highly expressive. Furthermore, inflection, emphasis, and many other expressive aspects of the voice are not a fixed part of our spoken language. Finally, words themselves, as verbal gesture, can by their meaning, arrangement, and emotional coloring be used to express emotion.

While it is generally true that nonverbal behavior accounts for the bulk of our emotional expressiveness, our verbal expression specifies our feelings and permits us to conceptualize about them. As such, verbal expression is a part of the whole expressive mechanism, and as far as the communication of feeling is concerned, our verbalizations are simply one class of gesture by which we make our feelings known.

Since the playwright has provided our verbal gestures in his script, the actor's creation is largely the nonverbal aspect of the performance—the physical gestures, posture, inflections, facial expressions, and so on. As we shall see in Part Two, the verbal language of the text is rich in clues about nonverbal gesture, but as far as the performance of a specific role is concerned, we must wait until we have learned the techniques of textual analysis. In a general way, however, we can proceed to explore the expressive possibilities of gesture as a means of communication.

GESTURE AND COMMUNICATION

Our culture has a large shared vocabulary of some types of gesture, which we use to augment our verbal communication. Some gestures have fairly consistent meanings when they appear in similar situations. Such gestures are symbolic expressions of feelings.

In its symbolic function, gesture provides a *physical analogy* for actions or feelings being expressed or described. While our *verbal* language provides a system for the communication of fairly precise meanings, our *gestural* language provides information about feelings and actions with greater expressiveness than words alone.

> Gestures achieve their highest degree of analogical value in emotional expression, but they also continue to serve as simple indicators in traffic, in games, and in love. Gestures have a communicative range from the universal down to the idiosyncratic; they may substitute for words or accompany words.[13]

---

[13] Bacon and Breen, *Literature as Experience*, p. 29.

Figure 6.   Three Illustrations of "Gesture Communication" Exercises.

Group Exercise 5: Gesture Communication
Scene

With a partner, decide on some important message to be communicated between you, and a reply. It should be about something of *vital* concern to both of you in whatever imagined relationship you establish. When you are both clear about the message and reply, the imagined relationship, and allowing for the possibility of communication that extends beyond the predetermined message and reply, begin to work out a dance-like scene in which you communicate the message and reply using *only* physical gestures and nonverbal noises.

Do not limit yourself to realistic movements or noises, and do not treat the scene as a charade. Your objective is not to make the message and reply clear as simple information; a few words would do that job much better. The gestures and noises are here not only a substitute for words, but a means of profound emotional communication. Your objective, then, is to communicate fully with each other using only the vehicle of gesture and noise; the information communicated is of secondary importance and only provides an occasion for the communication.

As you work on a scene like this, you may find it helpful to concentrate first on trusting each other as teammates. One device is to face each other, and after relaxing and placing yourselves in alignment, signaling your readiness to begin. Some groups have developed this procedure as a regular "clicking in," since the signal used is a clicking noise in the side of the mouth (like signalling a horse), and the process is used at the start of every group effort to insure the readiness of all the participants.

When, in your gesture and noise scene, you feel that honest communication has taken place (usually you will have been led beyond the original give-and-take to a further scene), present it to your audience, asking them to guess at the nature of the original message. Though the accuracy of their guesses is unimportant, their comments will be revealing about the quality of your communication. What did they find most "real?" Was the message-guessing or the contact itself more interesting?

CATEGORIES OF PHYSICAL GESTURE

We can divide the language of gestures into four broad categories of gestural function:

1. Illustrative, or imitative;
2. Indicative;
3. Emphatic;
4. Autistic.

Illustrative gestures are "pantomimic" in communicating specific information ("the box was about this high and this wide"). The indicative gesture points ("it's right over there"). The emphatic gesture provides subjective rather than objective information, relating how we *felt* about something (as we say "now listen here," we pound our fist on the table or jab our finger into our opponent's face). The autistic gesture (meaning literally "to the self") is not intended for social communication, but is rather a way in which we communicate privately to ourselves. Suppose that as I listen to you speak I have hostile feelings, which for some reason I must conceal from you. With my arms crossed over my chest, I am viciously clutching the flesh under one of my armpits. In this secret manner, I am having some symbolic satisfaction in strangling you, the flesh of armpit substituting for the flesh of your neck. While such gestures are usually hidden, they are often unconsciously perceived and recognized by the people around us.

Obviously, these categories are not distinct in actual performance and are for purposes of our study only. Almost every gesture we make serves a combination of two or three of these functions simultaneously.

Exercise 22: Physical Gesture Scene

Select a simple but highly physical action. Perform it four times, each time utilizing a different kind of gesture exclusively. For example, if your action is pantomimically to lift a heavy box and move it across the room, you would:

1. Illustrate lifting it, as if you were telling us about how you did it without actually doing it. You may use words as well as gestures here.
2. Indicate lifting it. ("I'll pick it up from over there and carry it over here.")
3. Use emphatic gestures that are *symbolic* (rather than illustrative) as you tell us *how it felt* to lift the heavy box. See especially how your voice is affected.
4. Finally, perform the action symbolically and *secretly* using autistic gestures (for example, hitching up your belt as a substitute for lifting the box).

Which categories resulted in meaningful involvement in the action? Do you see why indirect and highly selective gesture is often more effective and interesting than obvious pantomime or indication? What interrelationships in the kinds of gesture did you perceive?

**Exercise 23: Implied Gestures in the
                Script**

Notice how often the verbal language of a play's script makes demands of a nonverbal nature upon us. The following speech from *King Lear* demands gestures of all four types. Try performing it and seeing what kinds of gesture and what interrelationships of gestures are demanded. See how far you can go in physicalizing this speech, to the point of making it a dance.

> LEAR: When I do stare, see how the subject quakes. I pardon that man's life. What was thy cause? Adultery? Thou shalt not die. Die for adultery? The wren goes to't, and the small gilded fly does lecher in my sight. Let copulation thrive, for Gloucester's bastard son was kinder to his father than my daughters got 'tween the lawful sheets. To't luxury, pell-mell! for I lack soldiers. Behold yond simpering dame, whose face between her forks presages snow, that minces virtue, and does shake the head to hear of pleasure's name: the fitchew nor the soiled horse goes to't with a more riotous appetite. Down from the waist they are centaurs, though women all above. But to the girdle do the gods inherit, beneath is all the fiends'.

There's hell, there's darkness, there is the sulphurous pit: burning, scalding, stench, consumption. Fie, fie, fie! pah, pah! Give me an ounce of civet, good apothecary, to sweeten my imagination. There's money for thee.

This is only the most obvious way in which the verbal language can determine the nonverbal language of stage performance.

KINESICS

A great deal of study has been devoted to the verbal gesture and the whole system of verbal language. Until recently, the study of nonverbal gesture received little attention, but several physiologists and psychologists are now hard at work on the problem. This area of study has been given the name "kinesics" by Professor Raymond Birdwhistle. He defines this new field as "the study of body motion as related to the nonverbal aspects of interpersonal communication." Several of his basic premises are of tremendous importance to the actor:

A. No motion is a thing in itself. It is always a part of a pattern. There is no "meaningless motor activity."
B. Until otherwise demonstrated, body motion patterns should be regarded as socially learned.
C. No unit of motion carries meaning *per se*. Meaning arises in context. It is the physiological similarity of our bodies and the generally similar influences of our environment which cause many gestures to develop roughly standardized meanings within our culture.

Here is a brief example of nonverbal expression at work as observed by Professor Birdwhistle. He recorded this encounter (he calls such encounters "scenes") using his special system of notation for nonverbal action; luckily he provides us with verbal descriptions, which serve as stage directions.

The situation is that a guest of honor at a party arrives forty-five minutes late. Three couples besides the host and hostess have been waiting. The doorbell rings.

HOSTESS: Oh! We were afraid you weren't coming; but good. (As the hostess opened the door to admit her guest, she smiled a closed-toothed smile. As she began speaking she drew her hands, drawn into loose fists, up between her breasts. Opening her eyes very wide, she then closed them slowly and held them closed for several words. As she began to speak, she dropped her head to one side and then moved it toward the guest in a slow sweep. She then pursed her lips momentarily before continuing to speak, nodded, shut her eyes again, and spread her arms, indicating that he should enter.)

GUEST: I'm very sorry; got held up you know, calls and all that. (He looked at her fixedly, shook his head, and spread his arms with his hands held open. He then began to shuffle his feet and raise one hand, turning it slightly outward. He nodded, raised his other hand, and turned palmside up as he continued his vocalization. Then he dropped both hands and held them palms forward, to the side and away from his thighs. He continued his shuffling.)

HOSTESS: Put your wraps here. People are dying to meet you. I've told them all about you. (She smiled at him, lips pulled back from clenched teeth, then, as she indicated where he should put his coat, she dropped her face momentarily into an expressionless pose. She smiled toothily again, clucked and slowly shut, opened, and shut her eyes again as she pointed to the guests with her lips. She then swept her head from one side to the other. As she said the word 'all' she moved her head in a sweep up and down from one side to the other, shut her eyes slowly again, pursed her lips, and grasped the guest's lapel.)

GUEST: You have? Well, I don't know. . . . Yes. . . . No. . . . I'd love to meet them. (The guest hunched his shoulders, which pulled his lapel out of the hostess' grasp. He held his coat with both hands, frowned, and then blinked rapidly as he slipped the coat off. He continued to hold tightly to his coat.)[14]

As you reconstruct this scene in your mind's eye, it is obvious that the nonverbal behavior is very eloquent; moreover, it tends to express feelings that run *counter* to the surface meaning of the words being spoken. This is an extremely important aspect of nonverbal expression. It often "counterpoints" or even contradicts our verbal expression, and "safely" expresses feelings that situations force us to suppress.

We can deduce a great deal of information from the gestures recorded in the scene above. The "logic of the body" has, within our culture, provided us with certain conventionalized meanings, which are apparent within this scene. The clenching of the teeth beneath the smile, the making of fists, the shuffling of feet, all tend to have generalized meanings when they appear in certain situations.

Professor Birdwhistle is not the first man to engage in the observation and "decoding" of nonverbal behavior. Here is Sherlock Holmes in action, from "A Case of Identity," by Sir Arthur Conan Doyle:

> He had risen from his chair and was standing between the parted blinds, gazing down into the dull neutral-tinted London street . . . on the pavement opposite there stood a large woman with a heavy fur boa around her neck, and a large curling red feather in a broad-brimmed hat which was tilted in a coquettish Duchess of Devonshire fashion over her ear. From under this great panoply she peeped up in a nervous, hesitating

---
[14] Raymond Birdwhistle, *Introduction to Kinesics* (Louisville, Kentucky: University of Louisville Pamphlet, 1957), pp. 29–30.

fashion at our window, while her body oscillated backward and forward, and her fingers fidgeted with her glove buttons. Suddenly, with a plunge as of the swimmer who leaves the bank, she hurled across the road and we heard the sharp clang of the bell. "I have seen those symptoms before," said Holmes, throwing his cigarette into the fire. "Oscillation upon the pavement always means an *affaire de coeur*. She would like advice, but is not sure that the matter is not too delicate for communication. And yet even here we may discriminate. When a woman has been seriously wronged by a man she no longer oscillates, and the usual symptom is a broken bell wire. Here we may take it that there is a love matter, but that the maiden is not so much angered as perplexed, or grieved. But here she comes in person to resolve our doubts."[15]

In his book, *The Silent Language*, Edward Hall comments on this passage by saying that, "Sir Arthur made explicit a highly complex process which many of us go through without knowing that we are involved. Those of us who keep our eyes open can read volumes into what we see going on around us."[16]

Group Exercise 6: The Science of Deduction

Try playing Sherlock Holmes with the Hostess/Guest scene recorded by Professor Birdwhistle above. In a short, written description recreate, as imaginatively as you can, the backgrounds of the behavior of each; prophesy as well as you can the immediate future of their relationship. As a group, compare your accounts to see what similar deductions you have made. What areas were the most difficult for you to agree on?

Art has always been interested in "the silent language," and no art more than that of the actor. While the actor is very often interested in the unique, individual ("idiosyncratic"), behavior of individuals, he is also profoundly concerned with the aspects of behavior that are common within his culture. We can see the evolution of common nonverbal gestures growing out of actions that were at one time practical in nature. Man's present state of development has changed the needs of his behavior and has changed the purpose of much of his physical behavior. A situation that at one time had to be met with physical action on our part is now "solved" for us by our technology or more complex social structure. But the original behavior, in a reduced state, often persists. It is now purely expressive, and no longer functional. The way in which vestiges of physical behavior can live on as symbolic activity, even after the action has ceased to be practical, is explained by Charles Darwin in

---

[15] Edward T. Hall, *The Silent Language* (Greenwich, Conn.: Fawcett World Library Premier Books, 1959), p. 43.
[16] Hall, *The Silent Language*, p. 42.

The Expression of Emotion in Man and Animal, and expanded on here by Robert S. Breen:

> Consider the expressive value of behavior that was once in our human history adaptive, but is no longer so except in a vestigial sense—for example, the baring of teeth in the preparation for attack or defense. In primitive experience, the use of the teeth for tearing and rending an enemy was common enough, and a very effective means of adapting to an environmental necessity. Today, the use of teeth in this primitive fashion is rare, but the baring of the teeth is still very much with us. In an attitude of pugnacity, men will frequently clench their teeth and draw back their lips to expose their teeth. This action is a reinstatement of the primitive pattern of biting, though there is no *real* intention of using the teeth in such a fashion. The 'tough guy' talks through his teeth because he is habituated to an attitude of aggressiveness. When he bares his teeth, it is a warning to all who see him that he is prepared to attack or to defend himself. His speech is characterised by a nasality because his oral cavity is closed, and his breath escapes primarily through his nose. Lip action in speech is curtailed because the jaw is held so close to the upper jaw that there is little room between the lips for even their normal activity. Restriction of the lip action results in the tough guy's talking out of the corner of his mouth.
>
> When we see a person bare his clenched teeth, curl his lip, narrow his eyes, deepen his breathing, etc., we conclude that he is angry. These are the *signs* of attack in our ancestors which have become for us *social symbols expressive of an emotional state* known as *anger*.[17]

One of the first studies of the "silent language," which may have been influential on the style of acting of its time, was John Bulwer's *Chirologia and Chironomia*, written in 1644. The book calls itself a study of "the Speaking Motions, and Discoursing Gestures, the patheticall motions of the minde." The book discussed and illustrated (see Figure 7) an enormous number of feelings as expressed by nonverbal gestures. Attempts to categorize physical gestures for the performer and speaker were made throughout the seventeenth, eighteenth, and nineteenth centuries, and a few modern systems of acting use, in a very modified form, a formalized approach to the physical expression of emotion by locating "emotion centers" in the body. This is an approach also common to much oriental acting.

So far we have been talking about the ways in which we observe and interpret the silent language. But the actor must generate and participate in the nonverbal actions of his character. We should therefore explore, in a general way, how gesture is generated, and how the actor can control the process.

The main argument about the actor's creation of the externals of his performances is whether they should be treated as externals and approached

---

[17] Bacon and Breen, *Literature as Experience*, p. 32.

Figure 7. An Old Method of Indicating Emotion.

62

"from the outside," or viewed as the necessary result of an inner state and approached "from the inside." Rarely, however, is one point of view taken to the complete exclusion of the other.

Even a ridgidly "external" approach, as in the Kabuki theatre, takes into account the significance of inward states. Earle Ernst, in his book, *The Kabuki Theatre*, describes the oriental actor's attitude toward his character this way: "The approach of the Kabuki actor to the character is summed up in this practice: in the small room at the end of the *hanamichi*, there is a large mirror; when the actor is fully prepared for his entrance, he sits before the mirror and studies his figure so that he can absorb the nature of the character he is to play by concentration on its external appearance." But the Kabuki actor's job is only half done if he is satisfied with simple externals. Although the Kabuki actor does not "base the character on something within himself," he *does* derive "from the visual image an inward significance." In doing so, he follows the theory and practice of Japanese art. The poet Basho's advice to his pupils was "feel like the pine when you look at the pine, like the bamboo when you look at the bamboo." In other words, "truthful, artistic expression can arise only with the complete surrender of the artist to the nature of the object before him, a surrender uninhibited by the artist's intellect or emotions."[18]

For Stanislavski, this idea of the actor's surrender to his character was uppermost. The Kabuki actor achieves it by working from the "outside" to the "inward significance." Stanislavski achieved it by working from the "inside" of the character to the "outside." We often overlook the importance Stanislavski placed on the externals. Just like the Kabuki actor, he stood in full costume and make-up before a mirror, fully realizing his own externals before he considered his characterization complete.

Both approaches, reasonably used, are pathways to the same objective: critical control over externals supported by a vital involvement in the "inward significance" of the character. The first approach is lifeless without the second; the second is crude and ineffective without the first. In order to achieve both, we must discipline ourselves to avoid imposing aspects of our real-life behavior on our character, either in terms of nonverbal mannerisms or attitudes of thought or emotion.

Exercise 24: Putting Yourself in the Scene

Take the Hostess/Guest scene on page 58 and recreate it on the stage as faithfully as you can. This is not much different than doing a scene in which a playwright has provided extensive stage directions for the actor.

---

[18] Earle Ernst, *The Kabuki Theatre* (New York: Grove Press, 1956), p. 193. Used by permission of Oxford University Press.

Have those who watch identify mannerisms, inflections, and other aspects of your *own* nonverbal behavior, which appeared in the scene. Evaluate each to see if it contributed to our further understanding of the scene or if it introduced irrelevant or even contrary elements. Also isolate aspects of the character's behavior in the scene that were different from your real-life behavior. Did performing these actions give you special insight into the character? Did these modifications in your own behavior give you new insight into yourself? Examine those aspects of your real-life behavior, that happened to fit the scene, and those aspects that were most different from your real-life self. Which contributed most to the scene and your understanding? To improve the scene, which would you have to work on further?

THE "MASK" OF PERSONALITY

In the emotion adoption exercise (Exercise 14), you "put on" the externals of an emotion, as if they were parts of a costume, and worked for the internalization of the emotion. In Exercise 24, you adopted the externals of a person's behavior in a social situation. Did some of the person's attitudes and feelings grow within you? Did your participation in these externals develop greater empathy ("in-feeling") for you and the person?

When you read and analyzed the scene described, you probably felt vicariously some of the feelings of the persons involved; but you felt them through your conceptual understanding of the situation. Since your conceptualization was drawn from your own awareness and experience, you were responding not to *his* feelings, but to *your* feelings as they would be if you were in his place.

Now you have physically placed yourself in his place, and some of his experience is yours. What new insights did you gain? Did you begin to feel the character's inner state, or was it just your own translated into the character's situation, or a combination of both?

When you adopted the externals of the character, it was much like putting on a *mask*. If you put on a mask of a fat, happy person, you *look* fat and happy, regardless of how you feel. However, if you concentrate on your own appearance in the mask (like the Kabuki actor before his mirror) and begin to behave appropriately to your appearance, you will soon begin to *feel* fat and happy.

This seems well and good when we are talking about an actual, physical object like a *mask*, but what about the *personality* of a fat, happy person? Can you put that on and achieve the same results?

The word *personality* is derived from the Greek work *persona*, which means in fact, *mask*. Our "personality" is the "mask" or external image we attempt to present to the outside world. This "mask of personality" consists mainly of the gestures (in our broad sense of external signs of feeling) that are characteristic of our social self. Though our personality also consists of inner attitudes and feelings, which lie "behind" the mask, these "hidden" feelings develop and achieve importance of their own in relation to the mask of personality.

One theory is that the actor began, in ancient times, as a priest wearing a mask. He wore it as an act of worship, believing that by wearing the mask of a god, he assumed some of the power and identity of the god. Man still wears "masks" of various types and for the same purpose. Owning a Cadillac makes us feel rich, even if we're not. Smoking a pipe makes us feel mature, even if we're not. Waving the flag makes us feel patriotic, even if we're not.

So it is for the actor. Putting on the mask of the character's personality— if we honestly and vigorously meet the demands the mask makes upon us rather than attempting to reshape the mask to fit us—will help us to feel like the character.

Exercise 25: Masks

Buy or make some masks, each of a distinct "type." Wear a mask for a time, looking in a mirror. Move about with it on and try to behave totally as the mask demands. In a group,, improvise a situation (you can use the Hostess/Guest scene as a basis, if you wish) and criticize each other when you fail to behave as the mask.

Trade masks often during the improvisation. How quickly do you adapt to the demands of a new mask?

Repeat the exercise but use rigid facial expressions instead of actual masks.

Check your posture, your voice, your rhythms, your breath, and so on. Have you become *totally* involved with your mask?

While masks often have unique properties of their own. They usually represent some general *type* of character. The idea of "type" is very much in disfavor, both in theatre and in psychology, as hopelessly old-fashioned. We prefer to regard each individual and each character as unique and the idea of a "type" on stage today is synonymous with bad acting.

However, there *is* such a thing as "typical" behavior, and each of us shares, to some extent or other, in sets of typical traits, aspects of behavior that are common within our culture. We also, of course, possess uniquely individual ("idiosyncratic") qualities in combination with more typical traits. The trouble with a "type" on the stage is that it tends to disregard these unique aspects of behavior, and the results is a fallacious caricature, which is as unbelievable as it is dishonest.

Unfortunately, our reaction against "types" has been so strong that we have practically outlawed typical characteristics on our stages. We tend to think that if your Stanley Kowalski isn't a completely unique character with a set of idiosyncratic gestures never before seen on any stage, you are somehow less of an "artist." The fact that Tennessee Williams meant Stanley Kowalski to be typical of a large segment of American heterosexual society tends to be subordinated to the individuality of your performance.

It has always been a purpose of art to reveal significant recurrent patterns of human experience at the same time that it embodies these typical qualities in a creation possessing its own unique properties. Typicality and uniqueness are *both* essential to a dramatic character: typicality provides comprehensibility and relevance, while uniqueness provides vividness.

The language of gestures *is* a language in the sense that some kinds of gestures are *typical* within a cultural group. And just as we all have unique qualities of speech, so do we all have a unique way of using gestural language. This uniqueness will be partly determined by the playwright in his creation of the character, and will be finally determined by our performance. But underlying the uniqueness, we must not lose sight of the typicality of gesture, posture, and so on, since it provides the foundation upon which our physical characterization is built.

Group Exercise 7: Types

Make two groups of slips of paper. On one group, write a number of personality "types" (for example, milque-toast, bully, business tycoon, spinster, and so on). On the other slips, write emotions (for example, fear, jealousy, joy, and so on). Pick one slip from each pile without showing it to anyone else. Without time to think about it, perform the following pantomime, attempting to manifest both the type and the emotion: walk into the room, sit down in a chair at a table and eat and drink for a few moments, then rise and leave the room.

In discussion with the group, see what agreement there was about the physical type and the emotion portrayed. Try to isolate which aspects of the performer's behavior communicatied each of the impressions received by his audience. For example, "We knew you were a spinster by the way in which you sat up so straight on the edge of the chair with your knees tight together," or "I knew you were a successful man because when you walked into the room you didn't bother to look where you were going."

Then discuss the symbolic meaning of each of the physical details that led to these impressions. In the first example, "spinsterliness" was communicated by the knees being held close together, because of the modesty, the frigidity, and the sexual fear implied by that posture. Also, the fact that you sat on the edge of the chair with a stiff back showed that you weren't willing to conform to your environment (in this case the chair), and that your behavior remained constant no matter what your situation. Also the stiffness of your movements implied not only the stiffness of age but the intellectual stiffness of someone very set in her ways. For our other example, the fact that the tycoon walked firmly and without looking exactly where his feet were being planted showed that he was used to having his own way, and did not stoop to make many accomodations in his behavior for the sake of his environment; he more or less expected things to stay out of his way.

Pay special attention to the expressiveness of the eating and drinking you perform. Just as breathing is a way in which we take the outside world into ourselves, so is eating. The pattern of eating and drinking can be extremely expressive of the way we feel about life. The tycoon might tear at his food animalistically, "getting the most" out of life by taking what he wants forcibly. The spinster, on the other hand, might cut the food into tiny pieces, placing each one in her mouth and thoroughly chewing it, showing that she prefers to take her experience small and neat and in easily manageable portions. She doesn't want to "strain" her responsive system too much. Of course, not all women who sit up rigid on the edge of their chairs are spinsters, nor do all spinsters behave exactly this way, since their inflexibility may manifest itself variously. If we were to depend in the creation of our performance on such erroneous thinking, then we would be guilty of caricature, not the creation of charecterization. But as such behavior arises *in context*, it communicates because of its typicality, and provides a starting point for further exploration and development of more subtle, more unique qualities of character.

PHYSICAL CHARACTERIZATION IN THE TEXT

Playwrights are extremely sensitive to this type of information. Notice how specific Albee is in *The Zoo Story* about the ritualistic patterns of Jerry's behavior in the way he paces, and so on. See what his attitude toward food and drink is within the play. Peter also maintains a characteristic posture and pattern of movement, which has been carefully determined by the playwright. In these physical aspects, *The Zoo Story* is almost a *pas de deux*, a dance for two people. *King Lear* presents a beautifully balanced set of contrasts of gesture, for example, the hesitant, slight Cordelia and the husky, aggressive Goneril and Regan, and the constant contrasting of the disability of age with the vigor of youth.

Playwrights have always used the "silent language." The entrance of the blind Oedipus speaks more than all the words of the messenger who describes his blinding. Shakespeare's plays are filled with examples: Falstaff's fatness as an expression of his incontinent spirit; Hotspur's stuttering as an expression of his impulsive nature, which prefers action to words; the mad Lear and the blinded Gloucester coming together at the end of the storm, showing us the mental and phsyical agony of man in their two beings. The language of gesture is one of the most eloquent spoken by great playwrights.

Exercise 26: Physical Characteristics

As a group, select one character from a play you have all studied. Now, individually, make lists of all the clues to his bodily characteristics and physical behavior you can find. Check the author's preface, stage directions, descriptions by other characters, and characteristics strongly implied by his background, situation, or behavior. Now each make a second list that represents your continuation of the first. In the way an archaeologist might reconstruct a whole animal from only a few bones, try to construct a whole body *and qualities of physical behavior* from the given characteristics. Then compare your lists: did you each find all there was to find in the play? How much agreement was there among your imaginative extensions of his physical traits?

LESSON 6 *Vocal Gesture*

> Speech is more than sound: it is at once verbal and nonverbal. Speech may be viewed as primarily expressive movement, "gestured meaning," or in the most limited sense, mouth gesture. . . . When speech is expressing ideas, we are content to accept it as symbolic, but when speech is understood as an expression of the *whole* personality, we must recognize the importance of the mimetic features that are essentially nonverbal.[19]

The great emphasis our culture places on verbal expression makes us forget that the voice, apart from the speaking of words, is an integral part of our expressive mechanism. While articulated speech is a painfully learned ability, vocal expressiveness is instinctive. Yet we tend to be much more aware of formal speech than natural vocal expression. Actors suffer especially from this dictatorship of words, and are usually reticent to embellish their speaking of the author's dialogue with even the modicum of expressive nonverbal sound we use in daily life. This is unfortunate, since vocal sounds are an important type of gesture, and highly expressive of personality.

Vocal gesture is a symbolic, but nonverbal, expression of personality and emotion. Margaret Schlauch points out in *The Gift of Language* that, "We use these nonlinguistic means of conveying ideas, all of us, as an accompaniment to speech. A cry, a tonal inflection, a gesture, are means of communication far more universal than language as we understand it. They are, in fact, universal enough to be conveyed to animals as well as other human beings."[20]

The "universal" appeal of all gesture, vocal and physical, makes it of great importance to the actor. Even when our vocal sounds are articulated as speech, we should regard this not as a separate activity, but only a further extension of our expressive behavior. In the next lesson, we will discuss the articulation of words, but remember that from an expressive point of view the step from verbal gesture to articulated speech is not very great.

---

[19] Bacon and Breen, *Literature as Experience*, p. 298.

[20] Margaret Schlauch, *The Gift of Language* (New York: Dover Publications, Inc., 1955), p. 3.

VOICE AS AN ORGANIC FUNCTION

When we examine the physical process by which we produce sound, a rather surprising fact comes to light. As the linguist, Edward Sapir, points out, "There are properly speaking no organs of speech. There are only organs that are incidentally useful in the production of speech sounds."[21] All the organs directly concerned in the production of speech first evolved for some other, more "basic" purpose. For this reason, speech is called an "overlaid function."

Figure 8.   A Vocal Over-flow Exercise Involving Two Actors.

---

[21] Edward Sapir, *Language* (New York: Harcourt, Brace & World, Inc., 1949), pp. 8–9.

The organs of speech are related to breathing, eating, or both. The diaphragm and lungs evolved for breathing, the larynx for swallowing, the tongue, the teeth, and the lips for chewing, the palate for tasting. We have already explored the intimate way in which breathing and eating are related to the expression of emotion, and we can see that the voice is, in its physiological genesis, integrally connected with these most basic expressive functions. Because of the vast complex of muscles involved in producing the voice, and the vital nature of these muscles, emotion is immediately reflected in the voice.

The network of overlaid functions that produce speech are complex and far-reaching. Each of the organs used for speech depends upon a complex set of muscles for its operation. The production of speech ultimately involves the participation of the entire body. Radio actors were good examples of this fact. Though their audiences could not see them, they did not decrease the extent of their physical activity while performing. Quite the opposite. Since the audience was depending solely on the sound of their voice to create in the mind's eye a visual picture of what was happening, they usually over-emphasized the movement of their bodies while performing, so that the voice, coming out of a massive muscular involvement of the body, would "sound right."

GESTURE AS "OVER-FLOW"

Man's natural impulse is to externalize his sensations and emotions. In fact, these externalizations are an *integral part* of sensation. According to Sapir:

> ... the sound of pain or the sound of joy does not, as such, indicate the emotion, it does not stand aloof, as it were, and announce that such and such an emotion is being felt. What it does is to serve as a more or less automatic overflow of the emotional energy: in a sense, it is part and parcel of the emotion itself.[22]

There are two important ideas here: first, that nonvocal and vocal gestures result as an "over-flow," a sort of safety-valve action; second, that such externalization of our inner feelings are part and parcel of the feelings themselves. Ernst Cassirer, in *The Philosophy of Symbolic Forms*, says, "Even the simplest *mimetic* expression of inner process shows ... that this seeming externalization is an essential factor in its own formation."[23]

Exercise 27: Over-Flow

This is an exercise in experiencing the "over-flow" or "safety-valve" action of vocal and physical gesture. Using a speech expressing a violent emotion,

---

[22] Sapir, *Language*, p. 5.

[23] Ernst Cassirer, *The Philosophy of Symbolic Forms*, trans. Ralph Manheim (New Haven, Conn.: Yale University Press, 1953), pp. 178–79.

read aloud with full concentration, suppressing all vocal and physical gesture. Repeat it several times over; feel how the demand for physical and vocal gesture grows in you as an increasing tension. Force yourself to the point where physical and vocal movement must erupt as the natural result of these tensions. When it has erupted, explore the gestures fully; push them to an extreme. Examine how you feel and how you sound.

There is an old story about a highly mannered, flamboyant actress who gestured so violently that her movements ceased to have any organic relationship to the scene she was performing. The director tied her hands together with a string. "When," he said, "your impulse to move is so strong that you break the string, then you can." This is a necessary caution to you that the kind of gestures you have been exploring must grow immediately out of the demands of your scene. Our aim in these exercises is to lift inhibitions toward physical and vocal gesture, so that you can respond *freely* and *fully* to your text.

In the course of rehearsing a part, you should go as far as you can in exploring the possibilities of gesture and movement. Later on, the essential details should be identified and the performance economized. Unfortunately, beginning actors rarely go far enough in their exploration. Assuming that you properly analyze your text and respond intensely to it, the "over-flow" of your response should provide you with a wealth of sound and movement from which to shape your performance.

VOCAL GESTURE AS MIMETIC BEHAVIOR

Some vocal gestures have consistent and communicable meanings, and form a sort of sub-vocabulary. These are sounds that communicate thoughts and attitudes by symbolically mimicking an appropriate physical act, which "politeness" may not permit us actually to perform in the situation. Or, we may use a sound associated with an appropriate situation or sensation, or a sound that is abstractly "symbolic," like the suspended tone of the "vocalized pause" ("Its . . . ah . . . a question of . . . ah. . . ."), which symbolically asks the listener to "hold on now, I'll get it in a moment, in the meantime I'll make this noise to hold your attention while I think." Most of our mimetic speech sounds, however, symbolically imitate larger physical actions.

As with physical gestures, it is the common construction of our bodies that make these mimetic sounds communicative. You will remember Charles Darwin's explanation of physical gesture as a vestige of animal behavior;

he also believed that many vocal gestures were symbolic of general bodily functions, as explained here by Robert Breen:

> Darwin pointed to the primitive practice of children who expressed their dislike for someone or something by sticking out their tongues and making a sound something like a bleating sheep. Sticking out the tongue was for Darwin a primitive reflex of vomiting or rejecting something distasteful; so, too, was the sound, which got its peculiar vocal quality from the extremely open throat through which it came. The open throat was, of course, a feature of the regurgitation, or vomiting, reflex. It is interesting that the civilized adult will show his contempt or distaste in much the same fashion, though much repressed. We are all familiar with the tone of voice which we recognized as "superior" or "contemptuous" because it has that "open throat" quality.[24]

Exercise 28: Vocal Emotion-Adoption

Observe real life conversation, looking for vocal gesture. List three types: those that have consistent meaning in various situations; those that are expressive of individual personality traits, and those most influenced by emotion, situation, and age.

Using your lists and observation of someone's vocal behavior while experiencing strong emotion, create for yourself a vocal portrait of an emotion expressed in a certain situation by a person of a certain type and age. Now "put on" your portrait and perform it, as in Emotion Adoption (Exercise 14), until the vocal action spreads to the entire body and the emotion becomes self-generating. Repeat your exercise, applying it to the same stylized character you used in Emotion Adoption in a New Form (Exercise 15).

Concentrate your awareness upon the sound of the exercise. What is the relationship between the internal feelings evoked by the scene and their externalization in sound? How does the act of externalization in sound itself further the completeness of the inner sensations? How is character expressed by vocal gesture?

VOCAL GESTURE AS "OFFSTAGE" BEHAVIOR

Just as physical gesture can express suppressed feelings, which situations force us to conceal and which are contrary to the surface meaning of what we are saying and doing, so too can vocal gestures express such "off

---

[24] Bacon and Breen, *Literature as Experience*, p. 286.

stage" attitudes. Though the dictionary meaning of the words we speak imparts information of a factual nature, the *way* in which we speak them is far more expressive of the way we feel. The tone of voice usually recognized as "sarcastic" is one obvious example of our conscious use of vocal gesture to express ourselves. But there are many examples from our unconscious behavior as well.

If, for example, I am attempting to convince you that I feel strongly about what I am saying, I may increase the loudness of my voice, elevate my pitch slightly, and enunciate sharply, hitting the hard consonants as a sort of a vocal "pounding-on-the-table." But when I interrupt my speech to take a breath, the breath turns out to be a sigh that is very close to a yawn. I have unwittingly revealed that I am actually bored with what I am saying, and probably with you, as well. There is a kind of perverse honesty in people, which causes them to betray themselves in these small ways. It is like the child who crosses his fingers while telling a lie: because the deception isn't perfect, we have satisfied our private need for honesty. The actor can make good use of this fact by bringing normally offstage vocal behavior within the realm of his conscious control.

Exercise 29: Offstage Vocal Behavior

Examine real life conversation to discover examples of vocal behavior. Attempt to analyze the logic behind such behavior. What makes it expressive?

Try out some of the gestures you have observed by selecting a speech from a play and performing it so as to communicate the opposite meaning and emotional tone from that which was originally intended. Do this by manipulating your vocal gestures.

Try the speech as if it were delivered by someone of a different age, sex, or physical type from the original, using vocal gesture to make this substitution clear.

As you delivered the speech with changed meaning, feeling, age, and so on, how much of the original text's richness was sacrificed? How much did the text resist your substitutions? From this exercise, we begin to see how vocal gesture is a submerged part of a playwright's verbal design.

VOCAL GESTURE AS THE ORIGIN OF LANGUAGE

We turn now from vocal gesture to noise shaped into the symbolic sounds (words) that make up our language. Several theories about how language developed suggest that the conventional word-language evolved out of man's early vocal expressiveness. According to Cassirer:

> ... when we seek to follow language back to its earliest beginnings, it seems to be not merely a representative sign for ideas, but also an emotional sign for sensuous drives and stimuli. The ancients knew this derivation of language from emotion, from the *pathos* of sensation, pleasure, and pain. In the opinion of Epicures, it is to this final source which is common to man and beast and hence truly "natural" that we must return, in order to understand the origin of language. Language is not the product of mere convention or arbitrary decree; it is as necessary and natural as immediate sensation itself. Sight, hearing, and the feelings of pleasure and pain are characteristic of man from the very first, and so likewise is the expression of our sensations and emotions.[25]

Early theorists supposed that as our *mimetic* cries and grunts became "standardized," speech resulted. Although a great deal of mimetic speech behavior persists even in today's language, recent studies point out that the development of symbolic speech cannot be entirely explained in this way, and is a complex *social* process involving a continuing interaction between people that exceeds mimetic self-expression. "Gestures and cries," said philosopher John Dewey, "are modes of organic behavior as much as are locomotion, seizing, and crunching. Language, signs and significance, come into existence not by intent and mind but by overflow, by-products in gestures and sounds. The story of language is the story of the use made of these occurrences."[26]

In any case, the articulation of vocal sounds into symbolic speech is a highly expressive activity involving our total organism. The actor should remember that speech is a *physical* process whereby thoughts find their expression in muscular activity. As such, it is itself a type of gesture (an external sign of an inward state). This highly physical aspect of speech is especially important to the actor, since the written language of plays is only a representation of the spoken language envisioned by the playwright.

SPEECH AS DECISION-MAKING

As we form our thoughts into physical activity called speech, we perforce make a great many decisions that are expressive of our fellings and personality. The communal nature of our shared language determines to some extent the way in which we express ourselves and (since language is one of the principal vehicles of thought) the way in which we think. Therefore, the process of verbalization also expresses the way in which we react to our social environment.

This *active* nature of the process of verbalization is of prime importance to

---

25 Cassirer, *The Philosophy of Symbolic Forms*, p. 148.

26 John Dewey, *Experience and Nature* (LaSalle, Illinois: Open Court Publishing Co., 1925), pp. 175–76.

the actor. If we deliver our lines merely as memorized words, we deprive our audience of the living process by which those words came to be. The character's impulse to express himself begins in some felt need or reaction; as the words which he utters are chosen, as he shapes them into phrases and sentences, he is constantly making decisions about emphasis, emotional tone, and so on. These decisions reveal what is really important to him and how he feels about it, and it is this living quality of speech "coming to be" that we must communicate to our audience.

This, of course, does *not* require halting speech, slow tempo, long pauses, or muttering and mumbling, all of which are too often used as easy substitutes for an honest participation in the process of verbalization. The playwright will have given sufficient indications of the quality of the process in the case of each character. The style of the play will also suggest a characteristic verbal process: the ornate witticisms of Restoration comedy are formed by a quick, graceful process, a sort of verbal fencing match, while some plays tear chunks of speech out of experience in a clumsy, painful manner. "Stammering is the native eloquence of us fog people," said Eugene O'Neill.

One of our primary responsibilities toward speech on the stage, then, is to recreate the living process of verbalization in the way demanded by the psychological nature of our character and the style of the play. The script is both our starting point and our final judge. It is a finished verbal product, which we "take apart" in analysis to discover the process of its creation; then, by embodying this process in our performance, we arrive once again at a living expression of the text.

Exercise 30: Slow-Motion Verbalization

Choose a short speech and, after memorizing it thoroughly, perform it so as to expose the process of verbalization. Begin by physically portraying it in full dance-like movement, accompanied by full vocal sounds expressing the *impulse* to speak (though not yet actual speech); then, again portrayed in full movement and sound, allow the words of the speech to gradually evolve out of your movement and sound like a picture coming into focus. Do this with each phrase or sentence, after finding the germinal thought expressed by that group of words. "Search" for each word, letting it be formed out of the need to communicate an exact idea. Let your voice and movement also express your searching for, and finding, of words. Does a sense of character begin to emerge as you understand the choices that are being made during the process of verbalization?

The "process of verbalization," which we explored in this exercise, is usually described by the term *diction*, which refers to our selection of specific words to express our thoughts. As we shall see in Lesson 8, the playwright's choice of words for each character reflects his entire concept of that character. Our ability to revitalize the process by which the selection was made is crucial to the understanding and creation of our character.

LESSON 7

Voice Production
and Articulation

The articulation of vocal sound into English speech has evolved in a surprisingly rigid manner. Out of the vast range of sounds of which we are capable, only a limited number are utilized for speech. For example, all the sounds of our language are "expiratory," produced by outgoing breath. "Inspiratory" sounds are entirely in the realm of nonverbal vocal gesture for us (though some of the world's other languages use them for speech, along with clicking, whistling, and so on).

Our speech then, begins with outgoing breath, and it is with the breath that we begin our study of it.

BREATH SUPPORT

The system of diaphragm, lungs, and bronchial tubes acts as a "bellows" and influences articulation by providing or supporting basic speech sound as well as accent, stress, and changes in volume. As the force of the breath stream increases, there are concomitant changes in resonance as well. The actor must develop this system of breath supply. We rarely utilize even half of our potential reservoir of air, nor do the demands of everyday speech cause us to develop the muscles that activate this bellows system to anywhere near their full potential.

This "bellows" operates simply: as the diaphragm (see Figure 9) pulls downward in the chest cavity, air is drawn into the lungs. As it pushes upward, the air is driven through the bronchial tubes and trachea, through the pharynx (which houses a valve that stops foreign matter from entering the lungs and serves double-duty as the vibrator of our vocal instrument) and then into the throat, mouth, and nasal chambers.

The relative distance that the diaphragm travels and its responsiveness relates directly to our ability to "project" our voices, though several other factors are equally important. The actor must be prepared to project effortlessly in even the largest auditorium. In many theatres, scenes that are supposed to

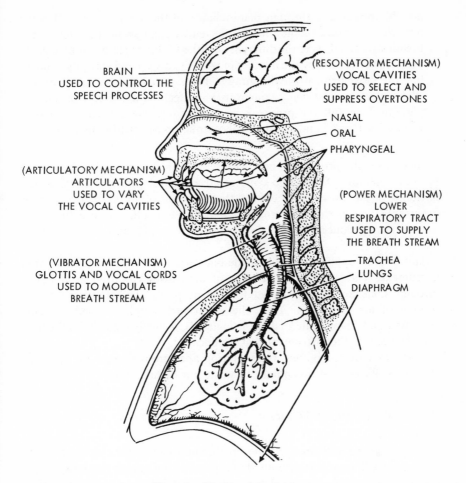

Figure 9. The Vocal Apparatus.

be quiet and intimate must be practically bellowed. Only the actor who can effortlessly provide the necessary minimum volume will be able to supply an illusion of quietness at the same time. Since there are a vast number of muscles involved in supporting the breath system, only massive, long range, and continuous exercise can develop you properly. Here is a simple exercise which can help you begin your development.

Exercise 31: Breath and Speech

In a standing position, place yourself at rest and in alignment. Produce a continuous vocalized tone and explore the variations in that tone that are possible principally through manipulation of the breath supply. Observe how the resonance of the tone is affected by changes in the force of the breath stream. Observe the different qualities of starting and stopping made possible in the tone by the manner in which you stop and start, by controlling the movement of the diaphragm. Place your hand on your stomach (the center area just *above* your waist) and feel the movement of the diaphragm. How full and precise is it? Is it unduly tense, causing its movement to be limited and erratic? Concentrate on eliminating tension here.

Set up a regular program of breath exercises, aimed at increasing the volume of your reservoir of air; also concentrate on developing the stamina and flexibility of the muscles that control that reservoir of air. Overbreathing, or *hyperventilating*, as well as timing how long you can hold your breath or how long you can produce a sustained tone, are all ways of judging your development.

This breath supply is utilized by the body just as it would be by any wind instrument. The outpouring column of air causes vibration as it passes through some aperture designed for the purpose. The vibration sets the column of air in motion. Thus, the vibration is amplified, and by being resonated and changed in quality (articulated), it finally emerges as the tone characteristic of the instrument that produced it.

In the case of our bodies, the vibration aperture is formed by the vocal chords. Inefficiency at this point can waste our breath supply.

TONE PRODUCTION

Without *both* an adequate breath supply and efficient breath utilization, you will be adversely limited in expressing the speech rhythms, phrase lengths, and expressive vocal tones demanded by your characterization. Unnecessary tension in the vocal chords and failure to utilize fully our amplifying and resonating chambers wastes our breath supply, no matter how fully we may develop it.

When we consider how the vocal chords operate, we see that they are capable of three basic types of movement:

1. When they are closed and tensed, the air stream is forced through them and they vibrate like reeds in the wind, producing tone. By increasing or decreasing their tension, we increase or decrease pitch.
2. When the vocal cords are drawn fully apart so that the air stream is permitted to pass through them unhindered, we produce the quality of speech called "voicelessness."
3. By a quick closing, the vocal chords can interrupt the breath stream suddenly and entirely, resulting in "glottal stop."

There is also a stage somewhere between the first and second, which produces a semi-voiced tone called "stage whisper."

Unnecessary tension in the throat area will adversely influence the operation of the vocal cords, and unnecessarily restrict the flow of breath. Under these circumstances, speech becomes an exhausting task. No undesirable muscular tension is communicated as quickly to an audience as tense throat. Actors have been known to perform with a painfully sprained ankle, with no one in the audience being the wiser; but a tense throat on stage results instantly in a wave of coughing from the audience. This fact demonstrates the strong communicativeness of our vocal quality.

The vocal cords are most involved in articulation by either "voicing" the breath steam or allowing it to pass freely as a "voiceless" sound. For example, *p* is a voiceless sound, while *b* is voiced. Otherwise, these two sounds are articulated in the same manner. Surprisingly, it requires more effort to produce voiceless sounds than voiced ones. Drawing the vocal cords fully apart is more difficult than allowing them to remain partly together, which is their normal position. You may have noticed that as you relax entirely just before sleeping, you sometimes produce a soft vocal tone as the breath flows through the slack vocal cords.

Exercise 32: Voiced and Voiceless Sound

Using the summary table of consonant sounds (Figure 10), explore the voiced and voiceless sounds. Do not move any part of the jaw, the tongue, or the palate while producing each pair of sounds, effecting the change only by drawing the vocal cords apart or allowing them to remain together. Hold a finger over your pharynx (your "adam's apple") and feel it change.

We have now determined the first way in which we articulate by producing voiced or unvoiced sounds. As the breath stream, whether voiced or not, passes beyond the pharynx, it encounters three further forms of articulation. First, the soft palate may raise or lower to direct the breath either into the nasal or the oral areas. Second, if the breath flows into the mouth, it is either impeded, or allowed to pass freely. Third, if it is impeded, the location of the point at which it is impeded produces a particular sound. The entire list looks like this:

1. Is the breath voiced or unvoiced?
2. Does the breath pass into the nasal or oral chamber?
3. If the oral chamber, is the breath impeded?
4. If impeded, at what point is it interrupted?

| POSITION IN THE MOUTH ⇨ | STOPS | | CONTINUANTS | | | | | |
	Voiced	Unvoiced	Nasals (voiced)	Fricatives voiced	Fricatives unvoiced	Blends voiced	Blends unvoiced	Glides (voiced)
Labial	Boy	Pony	Money	VERY	FUNNY	—	—	WOW
Dental	DOG	TOY	NONE	THESE ZOO (SIBILANTS)	THINK SORRY	—	—	LOVELY
Palatal	GEEK	KEY	CANYON	PLEASURE	SHE	JOYCE	CHOICE	RAT YES
Guttural	GUN	CUT	SING	—	HOT	—	—	—

Figure 10: Summary Table of Consonant Sounds.

NASAL SOUNDS

The first point beyond the vocal cords at which the breath stream is articulated is at the soft palate near the rear of the mouth. As this soft palate lowers or raises, it opens or closes the pathway by which the air stream may pass into the nasal cavity where it is resonated. In English we have only three basic sounds that depend upon nasal resonance: *m, n,* and *ng* (as in si*ng*). Nasal resonance plays an important part in causing the subtle variations of tone that produce the individual quality of our speech. Some regional dialects, as well as some speech defects, spring from the incorrect use of nasal resonance. As you perform these exercises, you may find defects or regional vocal mannerisms; you should do all you can to eliminate these inhibiting patterns of vocal behavior. If you have such a problem, seek out specialized training to help solve it. Few things can be as limiting to an actor as adverse vocal traits that are uncorrected.

Exercise 33: Nasal Sounds

While producing a continuous open tone (for example *a* as in f*a*ther), open and close the soft palate (turning the sound of *a* into *ng*), and concentrate your awareness on the vibrations produced in your throat, mouth, and in the area of your face surrounding your nose. Try this with a number of different sounds. While nasalizing, attempt to project the tone into the triangular area around the nose with such force that the surface vibrations in this area can be easily felt.

While producing non-nasal tones, see how much resonance the nasal cavity can provide *without altering* the basic quality of the tone. Check this by snapping the nostrils open and shut between your fingers. Projecting the tone toward the front of the face, producing strong vibrations in the nose and mouth area, or "mask," provides maximum resonance in the area of critical articulation.

ORAL SOUNDS: VOWELS AND CONSONANTS

VOWELS AND DIPTHONGS. The most complex part of articulation takes place in the mouth. The breath stream, voiced or unvoiced, may be either allowed to pass freely or impeded in some way. If is passes freely, it may be "shaped" by the positioning of the mouth's movable parts (mainly the tongue and lips). The sounds produced in this "open" fashion are, generally speaking, the vowels. The vowel sounds actually used in English far exceed the simple list *a*, *e*, *i*, *o*, and *u*. (See Figure 11). The four categories of vowels include those produced by shaping the mouth at the front (involving mainly the lips), the middle (using mainly tongue and lips), or back (using mainly the tongue and jaw), and those combined sounds called "dipthongs," which are unbroken glides from one vowel sound to another.

Exercise 34: Vowels

Place yourself at rest and in alignment, and using the summary table of vowel sounds (Figure 11), sing each sound in turn, concentrating on developing the fullest resonance possible and on efficiently using the breath supply. Are you getting maximum volume and resonance for minimum expenditure of air? Exaggerate the "shape" of the mouth in producing each sound. Read the lists in order, concentrating on the movement from front to rear in the mouth, and on the increasing "size," as more and more space is created within the mouth. Do the dipthongs in slow motion for a time to explore the gliding motion from one sound to another. Do you produce a clearly distinguishable sound for each type? As in your earlier vocalization exercises, a tape recording of your voice will be extremely useful in spotting any inefficiencies or peculiarities in your articulation.

FRONT VOWELS	MIDDLE VOWELS	BACK VOWELS	DIPTHONGS (*Glides from one vowel sound to another in a single syllable*)
WE	UP	CHARLES	MAY
WILL	FURTHER	WANTS	I
MAKE	FURTHER	ALL	JOIN
THEM		OLD	YOU
MAD		BOOKS	NOW
FAST		TOO	JOE

Figure 11. Summary Table of Vowel Sounds
Arranged from front to back in the mouth as you read down and across. Note that all vowels and dipthongs are voiced. Adapted from Evangeline Machlin's *Speech for the Stage* (Theatre Arts Books: 1966).

CONSONANTS. When the breath stream is impeded or even interrupted in the mouth, the resulting sounds are generally the consonants. The consonants are necessarily less resonant and more incisive than the vowels. "Consonant" originally meant "sounding with," indicating that these sounds alone cannot comprise a syllable; they must be combined with a vowel. While there are subtle exceptions to this rule, the consonants do serve, by virtue of their shorter duration and sharper tonal quality, as punctuation for the beginning or ending of vowel sounds.

When we consider the articulation of consonants, there are two principal questions: first, at what *position* in the mouth is the breath stream altered, and second, to what *extent* is it altered? In considering the first of these questions, we see that there are four principal positions within the mouth at which articulation may occur (see Figure 12).

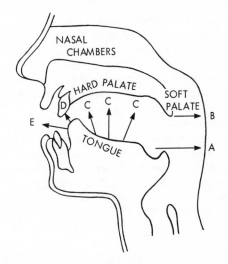

Figure 12. The points of articulation in the mouth: A. Guttural; B. Soft palate opens or closes nasal chambers; C. Palatal; D. Dental; E. Labial.

1. *Guttural:* the rear of the tongue may rise up to make contact with the soft palate to make sounds like "*g*un."
2. *Palatal:* a slightly higher sound may be produced by the middle of the tongue rising up to contact the roof of the mouth as in "*k*ey".
3. *Dental:* here the tongue is used in conjunction with either the bony ridge directly behind the upper teeth (as in the sound "*t*ea") or the teeth themselves (as in the sound "*th*ese").
4. *Labial:* the lips may be involved either by contacting the lower lip with the upper teeth (as in "*f*riend") or by having the lips contact each other (as in "*b*oy").

Notice that in each position different sounds are produced by either voicing or unvoicing the tone.

When we consider the *extent* to which the breath stream is altered, there are two main questions: is the breath stream entirely interrupted, or is it impeded but allowed to continue? When the breath stream is entirely interrupted, the result is called a "stop," since such a sound cannot be produced except for a short moment (*b*oy). "Stops" are also called "plosive," since they are produced by closing the breath stream off at some point in the mouth and then letting it "explode" suddenly. An impeded but continuous breath stream produces "continuants," so-called because these sounds can be held out over a period of time (b*oy*).

We now have two broad categories of consonants, *stops* and *continuants*. Within the general category of continuants, there are several subcategories:

1. *Nasals* (*m*, *n*, *ng*) have already been discussed.
2. *Fricatives* are produced by forcing the breath stream through a narrow passageway (*f*riend). Some (but not all) of these sounds have a hissing quality and are also called "spirants" and "sibilants" (*s*orry).
3. *Blends* are combined sounds produced by a plosive palatal sound, which blends immediately into a soft fricative or "hushing" sound. Examples are "*ch*oice, *J*oyce."
4. *Glides* are a momentary (and relatively slight) constriction of the breath stream, which immediately "glide" into a full vowel sound. Or, if the vowel precedes the glide, we "glide" into the constricted position. These are the "smoothest" of the consonant sounds and share some qualities of the vowels. Some of these sounds, like "*l*ove*l*y," are called "laterals" because the breath stream is blocked in the center of the mouth but allowed to flow around the sides of the tongue, or "laterally." Others, like "*r*at," are called "liquids," because there is only a slight constriction of the breath stream involved.

The summary table of consonant sounds on page 82 (Figure 10) lists examples of each; notice that nasals and liquids are always voiced, while fricatives and blends are either voiced or unvoiced.

Exercise 35: Consonants

Using the summary table of consonant sounds, explore the relationships between sounds. Exaggerating the motion or position involved, read in slow motion:

1. All labial sounds;
2. All dental sounds;
3. All palatal sounds;
4. All guttural sounds;
5. All nasals and glides;
6. All voiced and unvoiced pairs in the other categories.

Are you producing a distinctly different sound for each? Are regional peculiarities or bad speech habits affecting any of the sounds? Is the breath supply efficiently used for each? Are you getting maximum resonance from each?

Our distinction between vowels and consonants and some other classifications are simplified; today's linguists recognize a much more complex relationship between sounds. However, this simple classification system is sufficient to start us out on our long-range effort to develop efficient and flexible control of our articulation. Adequate vocal projection is not only a matter of strong breath support and efficient vocalization, but depends greatly upon efficient articulation. Many young actors think that being heard is a matter of speaking *loudly*; it is much more a matter of speaking *well*. The most common vocal shortcoming in the theatre, in fact, is the actor who can be easily *heard* but not easily *understood*.

ARTICULATION AND CHARACTERIZATION

As important as it is that you be able to speak "correctly," our study of articulation is really aimed at developing your voice as a *flexible instrument*, responsive to the demands of *character* and *style*. To achieve this flexibility and to be able to escape the speech habits of your everyday life, when necessary, the muscles that control articulation (like any other muscles) need exercise and disciplined development.

Along with the development of our control of articulation, we must develop our "ear," our ability to hear the expressive aspects of articulation in real life.

Exercise 36: Articulation and Character in Life

Observe around you the articulation habits of all sorts of people: how are laziness, timidity, audaciousness, and the host of other personality traits expressed in articulation?

What effect does a person's physical "type" and his dominant personality trait have upon his articulation?

What effect do phasic emotions have upon articulation?

As in the motion-adoption exercises, try to recreate articulatory patterns you have observed, and examine the feelings that result in your own being from these adoptions.

Situation has an enormous impact upon articulation. Since articulation is the muscular means by which we verbally present ourselves in society, it is extremely expressive of our feelings regarding that social situation. The emphasizing of hard, biting sounds may indicate one attitude, while the elongation and softening of open vowel sounds may indicate another. An evenness of accent and pitch may indicate timidity or a sense of represssion, while the voice of uninhibited joy may be extremely active in both range and dynamics. The host of expressive possibilities are subtle and complex, and deserve considerable exploration and study.

Exercise 37: Articulation and Character on Stage

Here is a prose speech from *King Lear*. Forgetting the actual meaning and function of this speech in that play, and the character who speaks it, use it for the following experiments. Again, a tape recording will help you immeasurably.

> These last eclipses in the sun and moon portend no good to us. 'Though the wisdom of nature can reason it thus and thus, yet nature finds itself scourged by the sequent effects. Love cools, friendship falls off, brothers divide. In cities, mutinies; in countries, discord; in palaces, treason; and the bond cracked 'twixt son and father. This villain of mine comes under the prediction, there's son against father; the king falls from bias of nature, there's father against child. We have seen the best of our time. Machinations, hollowness, treachery, and all ruinous disorders follow us disquietly to our graves.

A. Read the speech for "perfect" articulation. Exaggerate the sounds until your articulation is painfully precise. Read it as if this were not a sequence of meaningful words but only a sequence of sounds.

B. Read the speech again to express various emotions. What effect does anger have upon the articulation of these sounds? What sounds have been provided by the playwright to assist you in expressing anger? Likewise, consider the expression of fear and sorrow in the speech. Since all three of these emotions are present simultaneously in the speech as it occurs in the play, you will be discovering the sounds that the playwright provided as a means for the muscular expression of this compound emotion.

C. Read the speech as expressive of various dominant personality traits. What effect would timidity have upon the articulation of these sounds? Laziness? Pompousness? Stupidity?

D. What effect would situation have upon the articulation of these sounds? Read the speech as if it is a secret being communicated to a friend, then as a public statement being made before an immense crowd. Besides simple changes in volume, what other changes are there in your articulation in these contrasting situations?

Articulation, we see, is the muscular connection between *what* we say, and *how* we say it, since articulation is itself a complex gesture. Articulation of the sounds selected by the playwright is the first step in our muscular involvement in his play. From this involvement comes our sense of rhythm, vocal gesture, physical gesture, and all the aspects of the physicalized performance. As we shall see in the next part, playwrights, in the choice of words, create what might be viewed as a musical score filled with rhythms, sounds, dynamic markings, implied gestures—much of what we need in performance.

Playwrights write for the human voice; the human voice is deeply involved in the body's musculature; the body's musculature is deeply involved in our emotional life and thought. The playwright's words and implied actions provide, then, a direct route to a fully living, vivid, and appropriate stage performance.

OTHER IMPORTANT SKILLS

We have dealt here only with the most basic expressive skills of the actor. Advanced training in voice, speech, and movement, and in the generation and expression of emotion, goes far beyond what has been suggested here; and yet these basic skills and exercises will continue to challenge and benefit you for the rest of your acting life.

Seek out every opportunity to explore related training in such skills as singing, dancing, fencing, karate, and gymnastics. Each contributes in its own way to useful acting skills, and more importantly perhaps, to your contact and control of the body and voice. It is the practice of the physical and vocal *discipline*, presented in basic form here, honed and extended by advanced work and work in related fields, which liberates the actor's creativity; it disciplines his mind, his emotions, and his imagination simultaneously with its effect on his body and voice.

PART TWO

The Actor's Blueprint

The Aims
of Textual
Analysis

"Language," said Edward Sapir, "is the medium of literature as marble or bronze or clay are the materials of the sculptor." In order really to understand a dramatic text, then, we need to study the language, the words, which are the building blocks of the play. But since we are actors and not literary scholars, our reason for this study, and our approach to it, will be different from that of the English student. While he analyzes the text for its own sake as literature, we analyze it in order to solve the problems of "bringing it back to life" on the stage. This idea of rejuvenation of our text will be at the heart of our study of plays.

THE TEXT AS A RESIDUE
OF A LIVING VISION

The playwright begins by developing a living experience or idea, which we will call his vision. *It is this vision that moves him to create a specific work of art. Each character must come alive in the writer's consciousness. But, unlike the novelist, the playwright cannot usually speak directly to the audience in order to describe or qualify a character. The character must speak for himself; ultimately, the words spoken by the character will be all that is left (except for a few stage directions) of the fullness of the author's visualization. For the actor, then, the text is the* residue *of a living experience.*

We study the text in order to get back to the vision of which it is a residue. Remember, though, that this vision is not the same thing as the specific feelings and thoughts of the author. The good playwright transforms himself, submerging himself in his characters just as the actor must. The written text is an accurate record of this transformation and should be accepted as such.

The vision that underlies the text is something we can all share if we develop the ability to reach for it through the text. It is more basic than words: it is the power behind the words, a pre-verbal germ of communication.

REACHING FOR THE VISION

Since the vision drove the playwright to select and combine certain words in certain ways, to create certain characters in certain situations, and to structure the whole in a certain style, you can reach back to the vision best by analyzing these details, thus reversing the process by which the play was constructed. This is a more reliable and fruitful approach than simply trusting your own intuition or generalized response to the play. Many actors simply read a play and get a very strong feeling or intuition about it, which they then convince themselves is the vision behind the play. There is a great danger in working this way. While you certainly need to respond vigorously to plays, you must be careful to guide and correct your response by an informed and minute study of the details of the script. Otherwise, you have no guarantee that your response is really to the play itself and not merely to the personal feelings it may trigger in you.

Many modern actors, for example, have played Shylock, the Jewish money lender in Shakespeare's Merchant of Venice, *as a tragic hero, despite the fact that the play means to use him as a comic villain. This character was a stock figure in anti-Semitic Elizabethan England, and although Shakespeare humanizes the man more than his contemporaries did, the play still demands that he be a villain. Because we no longer share the Elizabethan's anti-Semitism, and especially since the events of World War II, most actors, Jew and Gentile alike (as well as*

most audiences), cannot separate their own feelings from the
reality of the play's structure. To some degree, this same sort
of "over-personalizing" has obscured or over-sentimentalized
many plays, including Brecht's Mother Courage, *Miller's* The
Crucible *and* Death of a Salesman, *Pinter's* The Caretaker,
and so on.

Moreover, each individual actor is often guilty of distorting a
role through over-personalization. A character like Jerry in The
Zoo Story, *for example, invites such strong emotional response*
from actors in their early twenties that it is very hard for them
to remember that he is supposed to be a man in his late thirties.
All sensitive readers have a personal relationship to a good
play, but the actor has the greater responsibility of presenting a
public performance of it. You owe it to your playwright, to
your audience, and to yourself to present the play for what it
really is, and not simply as a vehicle for your own feelings about
it.

SEEING THE WHOLE PLAY

Your analysis must take the entire play into account.
Dramatic characters are not real people; they are not meant to
be met as individuals. They are each created for a specific
purpose as part of a total structure, and they must interrelate
properly if the mechanism of the play's structure is to work as
it should. We cannot understand our characters if we don't
recognize the way they fit into the total picture.

Too many actors wear "blinders" and never see beyond their
individual roles. They behave as if they were spokesmen for
their own characters at the expense of a total interpretation.
This is a kind of selfishness that is deadly to the team effort
required by good theatre. You must respect the whole *play,*
not just your part in it.

This requires reading *and* studying *the whole play. Though*
this seems self-evident, many acting students work on scenes
from plays that they have only scanned. This kind of laziness
is encouraged by the fact that most acting classes work only on
individual scenes or speeches. Also, beginning actors
concentrate more on fulfilling each moment than on the shaping

of a whole role. Yet each word, each speech, each scene can be properly understood only *in relation to the whole play. If you fail to make this connection from the outset, you may become the kind of actor who has difficulty forming a meaningfully shaped and purposeful over-all performance.*

So, although the following lessons begin with work on individual speeches and progress to scenes, be sure you study the whole play carefully before you start work. Since you have no director now, develop your own basic interpretation of the play. Ask your instructor, or read commentaries on the play, to assist you in interpretation. Of course you will make many discoveries about the whole play as you work on each part, and in fact the only complete interpretation of a play is based upon such detailed study, but a good grasp of the play's outlines and a basic interpretation are possible and necessary at the outset.

Later on, as you work in productions, your director will help you and your fellow actors form an interpretation for the entire ensemble. Even if everyone involved analyzes the play carefully, there will still be some disagreement about the exact interpretation. This is so because a truly great play has many levels of meaning. King Lear *might be viewed as a play about old age, the responsibilities of kingship, the bond of love between parents and children, social injustice, or many other things. Even if you all agree that each of these interpretations is* part *of the play's total meaning, you must come to some agreement about the point of view or "focus" of your particular production.*

This focusing demands that each of your performances, as well as the setting, the costumes, and all the other aspects of the production, work effectively toward the total import of the production. The focusing of interpretation is the director's province. Even if your personal preference might be for a different interpretation or emphasis, it is still your job to work effectively within the director's production concept. If he has decided, for example, to do The Merchant of Venice *so as to make Shylock the hero, then it is your job to perform within his interpretation, even if you disagree with it. Remember that he is attempting to interpret the text in the way he feels will be most meaningful to your audience and will take the best advantage of the actors and facilities available. Thus, the responsibility for basic interpretation is his. But, within the bounds of a basic interpretation, you must minutely examine*

*your role in relation to the whole and grasp all that the
playwright has provided.*

THE ACTOR'S BLUEPRINT

*Just as there are several layers of meaning in a play that
operate simultaneously, ther are also several levels upon which
we can approach the analysis of the play. They may be described
as:*

1. *Diction:* the words themselves as chosen by the playwright;
2. *Melody:* the sounds and rhythms of the words;
3. *Imagery:* the sensations imparted by the words;
4. *Figurative language:* complex patterning of words to achieve special meaning;
5. *Dialogue* and *scene structure:* the patterning of speeches into units of action;
6. *Plot:* the linking of units of action into one basic movement, and the importance of the action to characterization.

*We shall examine each of these apsects of the text in the
following lessons, but as we do so, remember that each is only a
different point of view toward the same whole; a play cannot
actually be broken into parts. In analysis we take the play
apart to see what makes it tick; eventually we must reassemble
it in our performance, and make it run again "under its own
power."*

*We must synthesize what we learn from analysis in a unified
and congruous performance. Just as the carpenter or machinist
reads in his blueprint a detailed instruction for making an object,
the well-trained actor can read in a play specific clues about
rhythms, inflections, emphases, and all sorts of characteristics
needed to begin creating his role, if he learns the techniques of
analysis and applies them carefully and diligently. It is for this
reason that we call the play text the "actor's blueprint."*

POLARIZATION EXERCISES AND
SAMPLE ANALYSES

*As each lesson introduces a new aspect of text analysis, a
brief sample analysis of speeches from* King Lear *and* The Zoo
Story *will be given. Both these plays should be read carefully*

before continuing. These analyses exemplify, in a brief way, the principles outlined in the lesson; your analysis of a speech for performance would be much more thorough. The speeches to which all these sample analyses refer will be found on pages 100- 101.

Polarization Exercises

As we study each aspect of text analysis, you will be presented with an exercise polarizing that element of the text, an experimental performance that concentrates exclusively on some single aspect of the text. It will be especially interesting if you select a single solo speech, of one to three minutes duration, and use it for all six of the polarization exercises that follow. A speech from a great play with a strongly "poetic" content (whether it is in prose or poetry) would be the best choice. It should be thoroughly memorized before attempting the exercises, since they demand full concentration and complete freedom of movement. These exercises are not meant to be performances, but rather experiences for yourself. Each is a chance to take what you have learned from analysis of some aspect of the text, and turn it into movement and sound. In this way, your analysis does not remain coldly intellectual, but can be a meaningfully alive experience. Your objective in each, then, should be to find a pattern of movement and sound, based on qualities of the text, which will fully involve as many of your muscles as possible. Give the entire body a chance to participate. Never tie yourself to "realistic" movement, or even to the movement you might really use in performance. Rather, extend yourself to as active and as large a pattern of movement as possible.

While these exercises may sometimes resemble modern dance with vocal noises added, our interest is quite different from the dancer's. He creates movement for its own sake; you create it in order to provide yourself with a muscular experience, which brings some aspect of the text alive.

Don't let this personal nature of the exercise make you think that careful preparation is unnecessary, or that clarity and energy should be lacking. Think of them as a sort of interpretive gymnastics. Though you might never move this way if you were performing the same speech, it is important to let your body experience the fullest possible response to the text. The impulses

*to move that the body will remember will enrich your
performances later, even when extensive movement is not
actually involved.*

As you work on them, remember that you are abstracting,
*or removing from its original context, one aspect or another of
the speech. It may help you to begin work on each exercise
using the actual words of the speech, then "boiling it down"
to rhythm, melody, or whichever aspect is the aim of the
exercise. Of course, many of the exercises also use the words of
the original; follow the instructions in each case.*

*Advanced or more adventurous students may wish to select
a two-minute segment from a two-character scene to use in these
exercises, sharing the analyses in each case with their
partners.*

NOTE: this and the following page will be referred to often in the following lessons.

Speeches for
Sample Analyses

FROM **KING LEAR, ACT III, SCENE 4,** *BY WILLIAM SHAKESPEARE*

1. Poor naked wretches, wheresoe'er you are,
2. That bide the pelting of this pitiless storm,
3. How shall your houseless heads and unfed sides,
4. Your loop'd and window'd raggedness, defend you
5. From seasons such as these? O! I have ta'en
6. Too little care of this. Take physic, pomp;
7. Expose thyself to feel what wretches feel,
8. That thou mayst shake the superflux to them,
9. And show the heavens more just.

FROM THE ZOO STORY BY EDWARD ALBEE*

1. It's just . . . it's just that . . . (*JERRY is abnormally tense,*
2. *now*) . . . it's just that if you can't deal with people, you have
3. to make a start somewhere. WITH ANIMALS! (*Much faster now, and like*
4. *a conspirator*) Don't you see? A person has to have some way of
5. dealing with SOMETHING. If not with people . . . if not with
6. people . . . SOMETHING. With a bed, with a cockroach, with a mirror
7. . . . no, that's too hard, that's one of the last steps. With a
8. cockroach, with a . . . with a . . . with a carpet, a roll of toilet
9. paper . . . no, not that, either . . . that's a mirror, too; always
10. check bleeding. You see how hard it is to find things? With a street
11. corner, and too many lights, all colors reflecting on the oily-wet
12. streets . . . with a wisp of smoke, a wisp . . . of smoke . . .
13. with . . . with pornographic playing cards, with a strongbox . . .
14. WITHOUT A LOCK . . . with love, with vomiting, with crying, with
15. fury because the pretty little ladies aren't pretty little ladies,
16. with making money with your body which is an act of love and I
17. could prove it, with howling because you're alive; with God. How
18. about that? WITH GOD WHO IS A COLORED QUEEN WHO WEARS A KIMONO AND
19. PLUCKS HIS EYEBROWS, WHO IS A WOMAN WHO CRIES WITH DETERMINATION
20. BEHIND HER CLOSED DOOR . . . with God who, I'm told, turned his
21. back on the whole thing some time ago . . . with . . . some day,
22. with people. (*JERRY sighs the next word heavily*) People.

Analyzing the Speech: Diction

The vision of a great play is inextricably bound up with the exact words of the text. One of the things that makes a play great is language that has been so expertly used it becomes a part of the vision itself. As Sapir puts it, "In great art there is the illusion of absolute freedom. The formal restraints imposed by the material . . . are not perceived. . . . The artist has intuitively surrendered to the inescapable tyranny of the material, made its brute nature fuse easily with his conception."[27] If you doubt the truth of this, try taking a speech from a great play and rephrasing it in your own words. Even if, individually, the words have the same meaning as the original, the whole speech will not communicate the same meaning or feeling. In a great play, the words themselves become *part* of the vision. For this reason, we begin a study of our role by studying the words themselves, the play's diction.

The term "diction" is sometimes used to mean "enunciation, or manner of speaking aloud," but this is only its secondary definition. Its primary meaning, in the sense of "*diction*ary," is "choice of words to express ideas; mode of expression in language." The process of verbalization, which we examined at the end of Part One, is the sequence of decisions that results in word-choice or *diction*. Understanding diction is one of an actor's primary obligations, not only because it is a characterizational device, but also because we have a responsibility to our author and our audience to communicate the meaning of our lines accurately.

Remember Sapir's statement, "Language is the medium of literature as marble or bronze or clay are the materials of the sculptor?" Words, however, are basically different from the sculptor's clay or the painter's pigment. They have a prior meaning of their own, which is not completely determined by the way the artisan shapes or patterns them. Though the writer exercises considerable control over subtle shadings of meaning and emotional values of words, they present him with basic meanings of their own, which he must take

---

[27] Sapir, *Language*, p. 221.

into account. This basic dictionary meaning is called *denotation*. The emotional values that the words may generate are called *connotations*.

Until you have considered these two aspects of diction, the literal meaning and also the emotional colorings of the words of your role, you are not in a position to recreate the expressive process of word-choice or to proceed to a more detailed analysis of your text.

DENOTATION

It is suprising how many actors think they can get along on their intuition of the exact meaning of the words they speak. This is true of the actor who meets an unfamiliar or archaic word and "figures out" what it might mean from its context, and also of the actor who takes it for granted that he knows the meaning of words that "seem" familiar to him. When this happens, he may commit himself to a partially or completely erroneous line-reading without even suspecting that anything is amiss.

Meaning is not a static thing. There may be several possible definitions for a word. Also, the meaning of even common words in popular usage often changes quickly. Topical and colloquial speech may change its meaning very quickly, and doing a play only ten years old may require some investigation of the meaning of words and expressions. We must be sure that the meaning we take for granted today is not a distortion of the playwright's original intention.

Juliet, coming out upon her balcony (Romeo is hiding somewhere in the garden below) says, "O Romeo, Romeo? Wherefore art thou Romeo?" and many young actresses deliver the line as if Juliet were wishing that Romeo were there, in the sense of "Romeo, where are you?" But knowing that *wherefore* originally meant *why*, we see that she really is saying, "Why are you named Romeo, member of a family hated by my parents?" Such obsolete meanings are labelled "archaic" in the dictionary, and the intentional uses of an obsolete word is called an *archaism*.

One common way in which playwrights manipulate denotation is by *punning*. Though puns have been called "the lowest form of humor," they are used by great writers for both serious and comic effect. A pun depends on placing a word that has more than one denotation in a context in which both meanings could be applied. A "mark," for example, might be a marking, a bruise, or a kind of money. In Shakespeare's *Comedy of Errors*, a play literally filled with puns, one of the heroes has entrusted his money to his servant and later meets his servant's twin brother, who knows nothing about the money:

> MASTER: Where is the thousand marks thou hadst of me?
> SECOND SERVANT: I have some marks of yours upon my pate,

> Some of my mistress' marks upon my shoulders,
> But not a thousand marks between you both.
> If I should pay your worship those again,
> Perchance you will not bear them patiently.

From a modern source, we see the same delight in the possibilities of diction when we examine the names of Beckett's characters in *Endgame*. Hamm (ham), the decaying and impure meat and Clov (clove), the spice traditionally used with ham for flavor and preservation; ham is a meat that comes from an animal with a *clov*en hoof, and Clov is indeed the "feet" of Hamm; Hamm actor, the tragedian, and Clov (clown), who together are the two masks of drama and the two faces of mankind; Nell (nail), Clov (*clou* means "nail" in French), and Nagg (*Nagel* means "nail" in German) are pounded down by the overbearing Hamm (hammer); all are meanings wonderfully appropriate to the play.

CONNOTATION

The connotative possibilities of words are variable, unlike denotation which is much more rigidly determined by common usage. Therefore, we need to consider the context in order to determine which of the connotative possibilities are appropriate. In rich, skillful language, words will be selected so as to utilize more than one of their connotations, thereby supplying various levels of emotional impact.

Just as do persons in real life, dramatic characters use connotation as a way of revealing their attitudes and feelings toward something or someone. Connotation is therefore closely tied to the emotional life of the character. If the character describes someone as "swilling and gnawing and hulking," we understand not only her attitude toward the other person, but also something about the character herself, because of the way she has chosen to express her attitude.

As in the preceding example, the sensations that words evoke is an important part of connotation and demand from the actor a strongly physical response. The physical qualities of "swilling," and so on, should be forcefully suggested by the line delivery, and will heighten the emotional expression. When we understand our character's attitudes and feelings as they are revealed in connotation, we will possess a source of vivid physicalization of his emotional life.

PARAPHRASE

The problems of diction in old or modern plays are not restricted to puns, archaisms, or colloquialisms. They encompass our whole understanding of what we are saying in its historical, social, and psychological context. As we consider the words we speak, we must answer each of these questions: 1) *What were the meanings of the words when the play was written?* 2) *What do they mean when used by the kind of character we are playing?* 3) *What "hidden" meanings or references might there be in them?* 4) *How might any or all of these meanings operate in this context?*

One very good way to be sure we have asked ourselves the proper questions about diction is to *paraphrase*. This is the practice of restating the meaning of our lines in our own words. Going carefully, word by word and sentence by sentence over your lines, try to reword what the author has given you. Obviously, much of the emotional tone, the connotations and mood, and the poetic richness of the original will be destroyed. But even this will make us appreciate the subtleties of the author's language, and we will at least have made sure that we have considered seriously the possible meanings of each word we speak.

Good dictionaries will help you to be sure about diction. For modern plays, the Merriam-Webster dictionaries based on either their second or third unabridged editions as well as a dictionary of slang will be useful. For old (English) plays, the *Oxford English Dictionary* (the *O.E.D.*) lists the changing meanings of words with the dates of their currency. There are carefully noted editions of great classical plays with glossaries, or with a "running gloss." There are *variorum* editions of Shakespeare's plays, with explanatory notes and excerpts from important critical commentary, line by line.

SYNTAX

Syntax refers to "the due arrangement of word forms to show their *mutual relation* in the sentence." This idea of "mutual relation" is expressed in an old theatrical maxim that a good delivery of a line will "throw away" or de-emphasize 80 percent of the words in order to give the proper emphasis to the remaining 20 percent in which the meaning is crystallized. This is only to say that the intelligibility of our speech depends more on the "shape," patterning, or mutual relation of words than on the meaning of individual words.

It is the nature of our language that "idea units" (sentences or independent phrases) have, to some extent, a conventional structure that provides unity and focus. Playwrights may also achieve unusual effects by departing from traditional structures and employing inverted or other unusual syntax. The emphasis that is directed to certain elements of the sentence, either by traditional or unusual structure, must be reflected in our delivery if we are to be faithful to the *phraseology* of the author.

In music, instrumentalists are often told by their teachers, "Don't play the notes, play the music!" This means understanding the shape and sense of a whole phrase, or section, as a unit and not simply as a sucession of individual notes. The actor's problem in the delivery of lines is like the musician's problem of phraseology. It is from the shaping of the larger thought units, phrases, sentences, and paragraphs that meaning best emerges. There are two basic types of syntax: *periodic* and *nonperiodic*.

In periodic structures, the sense of the idea unit is suspended throughout its length. The various elements "pile up" upon each other until the fullness of meaning is revealed at the end. This structure is particularly appropriate to the painting of word-pictures, where the total effect is achieved through a "funding" or combining of a number of descriptive elements. An excellent example of periodic structure, especially in its ability to create a funded verbal picture, comes from this description of Cleopatra's barge as it sails down the Nile in *Antony and Cleopatra*:

> The barge she sat in, like a burnish'd throne,
> Burn'd on the water. The poop was beaten gold;
> Purple the sails, and so perfumed that
> The winds were love-sick with them; the oars were silver,
> Which to the tune of flutes kept stroke, and made
> The water which they beat to follow faster,
> As amorous of their strokes.

Nonperiodic structures are less formal, more "conversational." One form of nonperiodic structure is the *balanced* sentence. Here, relatively self-sufficient elements of the sentence are juxtaposed and meaning is revealed by contrast. The contrasted elements need not be opposite to one another, only different. You can see this sort of structure at work in this famous speech by Marc Antony from *Julius Caesar*:

> Friends, Romans, countrymen, lend me your ears;
> I come to bury Caesar, not to praise him.
> The evil that men do lives after them;
> The good is oft interred with their bones;
> So let it be with Caesar. The noble Brutus
> Hath told you Caesar was ambitious.
> If it were so, it was a grievous fault;
> And grievously hath Caesar answer'd it.

SAMPLE DICTION ANALYSES

(Refer to sample speeches, pages 100-101)

KING LEAR. The periodic syntax of the first four lines develops a vivid cumulative picture of poverty. *Poor* in the first line is not simply a term of pity, but refers literally to those who suffer poverty. The theme of the

speech is economic and social injustice. The plight of the poor is made vivid
by highly physical connotations. *Wretch* originally referred to an exile who
had been driven out of his native country, so *wretches* are not only unfortunate persons but also those who are helpless and alone. The poor are, in this
sense, disenfranchised as well as miserable. To *bide* or "abide" connotes not
only endurance but a sense of expectation, the poor waiting to be lifted out of
their misery. The *pitiless* storm in which Lear finds himself also comes to
signify the pitilessness of society toward the poor. Lear makes it clear that he
refers not only to his own actual storm, but to the pitiless storm of human life
as well, when he ways "whereso'er you are" (whether you are in *my* storm or
not). *Pity* also connotes *piety* or moral rightness, a quality therefore lacking
in Lear's society. *Loop'd and window'd raggedness* depicts the holes in the
clothing of the poor and refers us back to *naked*.

The physical connotations of all these words develop a feeling of defense-
lessness, exposure to the elements, and helplessness, as well as a sense of
spiritual desolation. In line 6, he suggests the remedy: *Take physic, pomp*.
Pomp refers to the vain splendor of the rich, and *Take physic* connotes that
this concentration of riches is a disease that must be cured. *Physic* in the sense
of *physician* refers to healing and especially the giving of purges or enemas.
The image of *pomp* taking *physic* graphically reveals how Lear feels about the
rich as well as the way in which wealth needs to be dislodged and allowed to
flow freely to all levels of society. This image is supported by *shake the super-*
flux to them, which means "scatter your surplus wealth to the poor." *Shake*
also gives the physical connotation of shaking a tree so that the ripe fruit fall
out of it to be eaten.

In the last line, Lear suggests that *heaven* would appear more *just* if man
treated man humanely.

A paraphrase of this speech might look like this:

1. Poverty-striken, defenseless, and helpless people, whether you are in this
   actual storm or not,
2. Who are awaiting the end of this inhuman and unjust misery,
3. How will you be able, without adequate shelter and food,
4. With your tattered clothing, to withstand
5. This incessant deprivation? I was once rich, a king, in a position to help,
6. And I was blind to your plight. The splender of the rich must be dislodged;
7. The wealthy must open their hearts to the suffering of the poor,
8. And redistribute the excess wealth now in the hands of the few,
9. And thereby make the universe appear fairer than it does now.

A paraphrase, especially of poetry, will usually be much longer than the
original. Your aim is to make the *implied* meanings *explicit*. The words of
the original have been compacted until their meaning is distilled or intensified. To be sure you aren't missing anything, expand the speech into more

prosaic language. This will also help you to realize the economy of the original, the "rightness" of every word in every place.

THE ZOO STORY. "Realistic" prose is often less compact than poetry, but none the less rich. At the beginning of this speech, the diction is almost severe in its stark, straightforward simplicity. Around line 14, however Jerry has "tuned in," and his thoughts begin flowing in longer phrases, an outpouring of pent-up frustrations, the connotations becoming richer and more physical.

In lines 1-3, he is trying to get started, searching for a way of explaining his problem. In line 4, he begins enumerating the things he has tried to relate to, and he is soon describing his world, the world of his rooming house and apartment. The theme of *coping*, of "dealing" with things recurs, and the connotations of most of the words reflect a sense of basic physical inhibition, which relates to the search for identity through contact with others. The important thing about the pornographic playing cards in line 13 is that they are associated with an *unlocked* strongbox (they are a form of sexual contact that is accessible). In the next phrases, *love* triggers a sequence of *vomiting* (symbolic rejection of nourishing contact with life), *crying* (a vocal gesture of frustration in this context), *fury* over the disappointment of the realities of sex, the exaltation of the love act as transcendent of the circumstances in which it occurs, and *howling because you're alive* as the ambivalent awareness of the pain of existence (compare Lear's "Howl, howl, howl, howl.").

Finally, God, who symbolizes for Jerry contact between people, is connected to *A COLORED QUEEN* (a Negro homosexual), who, as a symbol of unnatural sexual contact, is preoccupied with maintaining a false illusion of femininity by plucking his eyebrows, and *A WOMAN WHO CRIES WITH DETERMINATION*, whose sorrow has become the only possible aggressive, *determined*, self-expressive gesture toward life behind *HER CLOSED DOOR*. Jerry's inability to open his door to human contact will lead him to his final, desperate act, a physical and strongly sexual contact through the knife.

Exercise 38: Diction Polarization

Study your selection, asking the four basic questions about diction, and analyzing it as in the examples. Write a line-by-line paraphrase of the speech. Re-read the instructions for these exercises on p. 98, then:

> 1. Deliver it slowly with descriptive gestures, so that you make the exact *denotations* of the speech painfully clear, and exaggerating the placement of emphasis suggested by the syntax.

2. Perform it again in a free-flowing, dance-like manner, emphasizing emphatic and suggestive gestures, attempting to communicate vividly the *connotations* of the speech.
3. Seriously perform your paraphrase as if it were the original. Compare the meaning and emotional quality that results from this performance with the original. What has been lost, and why? What has been gained, and how might it be kept in your performance of the original?

LESSON 9

Analyzing the Speech: Rhythm

Rhythm is not just a matter of the tempo of the speech (fast or slow) or the basic rhythm or "beat" of the speech, but also the variation of tempo and beat that provides *emphasis*. In good writing, rhythm has been carefully controlled to provide a many-leveled or "contrapuntal" texture. Rhythm provides emphasis by *contrast*; the variations from the basic rhythm of a speech provide emphasis and focus on certain words, images, or other elements of the speech, and therefore contribute to the communication of meaning.

Besides supporting meaning through emphasis, rhythm is also expressive of emotion and personality. Many emotions have recognizable rhythmic qualities. When we are excited, for example, the tempo of our speech tends to increase and to become erratic and uneven. Likewise, various personality types are associated with characteristic rhythms. The blustery, pompous man has a rhythm of speech much different from the thoughtful, introspective man. Even nationality and social background affects rhythm. The Irish tend to speak each thought on one long exhalation of breath, imparting an unmistakeable rhythm to their speech. While in real life there are many exceptions to these stereotypes, playwrights nevertheless supply built-in rhythms that are appropriate to the establishment of a character's personality and emotion. Analysis of those rhythms may aid us in forming our characterization.

RHYTHM AND EMOTION

As we have already learned, emotion causes measurable changes in the tension of our muscles. This tensing of the muscles has a direct effect on our speech. In Lesson 4 we analyzed the muscular effects of anger as an example, and among its symptoms were several related to speech: tension in the diaphragm limits its movement, making us take shallow breaths. Since we need to oxygenate the muscles for defense purposes, we compensate by taking more rapid breaths. This causes us to break our speech up into shorter breath-phrases and to increase its tempo. Tension, spreading to the pharynx, causes an elevation of pitch, and coupled with the increased pressure of the breath stream, this results in a "punching" delivery and increased volume. The vestigal biting and tearing of the jaw related to anger encourages us to emphasize hard consonant sounds and our speech may become, in rage, similar to the snapping and growling of the angry animal.

This very basic example will remind you that both tone and rhythm are tied to our emotional state by the muscles that produce speech. By understanding the rhythms and tones our playwright has supplied for us and by experiencing them in our own muscles as we pronounce them, we will have a better chance of recreating the feelings they express. The next lesson will deal with tone, and it is rhythm and tone *together* that make the music of speech. For now we study rhythm for two reasons: to help us understand and support the meaning of the lines through the proper placement of emphasis, and to give us yet another tool for entering into the feelings of our character.

RHYTHM IN POETRY: SCANSION

We will turn first to the analysis of rhythm in poetry, since it is more formal than prose rhythm and analyzing it requires various special terms and techniques. The heightened patterning of rhythm in poetry is both a help and a hindrance to us: on the one hand it makes our analysis and delivery of the speech more complex, but on the other hand, it allows our analysis to be more orderly and specific than an analysis of prose rhythms can be. Nevertheless, rhythm is as carefully structured by good prose writers as it is by poets, and most of the *principles* of poetry analysis are also applicable to prose.

The general term for the patterning of poetic elements is *prosody*, and the name for analyzing rhythm syllable-by-syllable is *scansion*. Any word is made up of syllables, some of which are emphasized or *stressed* and some of which are unstressed. When these words are joined into a poetic line, their stressed and unstressed syllables work together to form an over-all pattern for that line. The first step in scanning a line is to identify the stressed and unstressed syllables. Take this famous line from *Romeo and Juliet* for example:

But soft! What light through yonder window breaks?

We know, first of all, that the pronunciation of multi-syllabled words determines the placement of some stresses, and we put a line called a *machron* ($-$) over the stressed syllables and a semicircle called a *breve* ($\smile$) over the unstressed ones.

But soft! What light through $\overline{\text{yon}}$der $\overline{\text{win}}$dow breaks?

Filling in the rest, we see this pattern emerge as we place other stresses demanded by meaning and syntax:

But soft! What light through yonder window breaks?

Though we have marked syllables as either stressed or unstressed, these are only very general categories, and there is actually a great deal of variation within each. If we were to read all stressed syllables one way and all unstressed another, the result would be a monotonous sing-song. Only a few of the stresses in each line are actually *major* stresses. In this line, for example, we would probably read only *soft! light*, and *breaks* as major stresses. At the same time, an unstressed syllable like *What* receives more emphasis than one like *der*. Nevertheless, a general pattern of alternating stressed and unstressed syllables can be recognized.

This pattern can be identified by using the most common system of English scansion, *foot scansion*. In foot scansion, the stressed and unstressed syllables are arranged into units called "feet." There are a limited number of these arrangements of stressed and unstressed syllables established by tradition. They work very much like measures in music. If I write |♩ ♩ ♩|, you recognize it as a measure of waltz time. The same is true of our arrangement of syllables. If I write | But, soft!|, it is recognized as a single *foot* called an *iamb*. The traditional feet used in English verse are six in number and look like this:

$$ \smile\smile\,|\,\smile - |- \smile\,|\,\smile\smile - |- \smile\smile\,|\,--\,| $$
$$ \text{P} \qquad \text{I} \qquad \text{T} \qquad \text{A} \qquad \text{D} \qquad \text{S} $$

You can remember their names by remembering the nonsense word PITADS. The first letter of PITADS, *P*, stands for the weakest and smallest foot, the *pyrrhic*, which has only two unstressed syllables | ⌣ ⌣ |. The second letter, *I*, stands for the most common foot, the *iambic*, which has an unstressed syllable followed by a stressed one | ⌣ — |. The third letter, *T*, stands for *trochaic*, the opposite of the *iambic* | — ⌣ |. *A* is for *anapestic*, which is different because it has three syllables, two unstressed and one stressed | ⌣ ⌣ — |. *D* is for *dactylic*, the opposite of the anapestic | — ⌣ ⌣ |. Finally, *S* is for *spondaic*, the strongest foot of all, with two stresses | — — |. If we look again at our line from *Romeo amd Juliet*, we see that it divides regularly into iambic feet:

But, soft! | What light | through yon | der win | dow breaks? |

The division of feet does not necessarily coincide with the division of words, and this is the first source of the contrapuntal quality of poetic meter. The *basic rhythm* or *meter* of alternating stressed and unstressed syllables goes against the natural pauses between words in some cases. This creates a contrapuntal tension, and there is usually a reason for this: either some particular part of the line, image, or idea is emphasized by the irregularity, or as in this example, a series of words are tied together. By deemphasizing the pauses between the words *through, yonder,* and *window,* the poet encourages us to speed over this section of the line. This helps shape the meaning of the whole by leaving more time for the key words *soft, light,* and *breaks.* Notice that you could say these three words alone in such a way as to communicate the sense of the entire original line.

We now know that our line is comprised of iambic feet, and we see that there are five feet in all. We can name this meter "iambic five-meter," or *iambic pentameter.* If there had been more or less than five feet, we would have named it dimeter (2), trimeter (3), tetrameter (4), hexameter (6), or heptameter (7). We identify the meter *by combining the name of the predominant kind of foot with the average number of feet per line,* Trochaic tetrameter, for example, would be a meter that *generally* had four trochaic feet in each line.

The iambic line has an impetus from the unstressed syllables leading up to the stressed ones and is called *rising meter.* A trochaic line has the opposite tendency, and is called *falling* meter. It is sometimes used to express sadness, as when King Lear, with his dead daughter in his arms, says:

> She'll come no more,
> Never, | never, | never, | never, | never. |

Iambic pentameter is the most common English meter. When it doesn't rhyme, iambic pentameter is called *blank verse.*

METRICAL VARIATIONS

We name poetry by the *dominant* kind of meter it possesses, expecting that there will be many variations. For example, we call Shakespeare's poetry blank verse or iambic pentameter, even though there are some lines with less or more than ten syllables and there are many feet that are not iambic.

Some variations are more common than others. In *Romeo and Juliet,* Juliet exclaims:

> Gallop apace, you fiery-footed steeds!

If we scan for pronunciation and meaning, we get:

> Gallop apace, you fiery-footed steeds!

When we divide this into feet, we get:

$$— \cup \, | \, \cup — \, | \, \cup — \, | \, \cup \, \cup — \, | \, \cup — \, |$$

Two irregularities are immediately obvious. The first foot isn't iambic, it is trochaic. This is an *inverted first foot* (since a trochee is an inverted iamb) and is a common variation. (It is also fairly common to find a spondee in the first foot.) The fourth foot is also not iambic, but anapestic. There is a great deal of argument about whether three-syllable feet (the anapest and dactyl) are "proper" in English poetry. Most critics feel that they are not, and that the poet wanted the line read to conform to the two-syllable pattern demanded by convention. Nevertheless, we ought to determine each case on its own merits, not by an all-inclusive rule.

If you pronounce all three syllables in *fiery*, you find that it stands out somewhat from the dominant meter. Your impulse is to speed up the word and compact these two syllables into the time taken by one of the other unstressed syllables, thereby keeping the basic beat of the line regular. This speed is certainly appropriate to the meaning of "fiery" and the image of which the word is a part, and this analysis might be a good argument for "leaving in" the extra syllable. If we do, the line has one syllable more than the basic ten syllable pattern and is called *hypermetrical.*

On the other hand, many scholars would say that this extra syllable should be "taken out" so that the line becomes regular. This can be done by the process of *elision*. You *elide* a syllable by slurring or gliding over it, so that it is *minimized* or eliminated altogether. You can see that it is quite easy to glide over the middle syllable of *fiery* and say the word as if it had only two syllables, *fi-ry*. If you do this, the meter of the line becomes regular. One of the best arguments in favor of such an elision is that the words containing hypermetrical syllables are usually easy ones to elide, and so must have been chosen for this purpose by the poet. Theatrical tradition is also in favor of making these elisions.

Elision is sometimes marked by the printer, and sometimes not. When you see a word printed "Heav'n" it may or may not be a proper elision. Only your own analysis will tell you, because these typographical markings were rarely made by the playwright himself.

Occasionally, we encounter a line which appears to have one syllable too few. Such a line is called *catalectic:*

> Now, | until | the break | of day, |
> Through | this house | each fai | ry stray. |

When we encounter a "missing" syllable, such as the absent first syllable in these lines from *A Midsummer Night's Dream*, our impulse in reading is to take a "rest," a beat of silence, where the missing syllable would normally be. In this example, the poet has used this device in order to emphasize the rhyming words at the end of each line by having them followed by a pause.

SHAPING OF POETIC LINES

We now have identified sources of contrapuntal levels of poetic rhythm, which involve individual syllables and words. There is a larger rhythmic pattern achieved by the over-all shaping of poetic lines.

A strong pause that interrupts a poetic line is called a *caesura*. It may be marked by a comma (though not all commas are caesuras), a semicolon, colon, or period. Often it won't be marked by punctuation at all, but only implied by syntax and sense.

Poor na|kĕd wre|tchĕs, where|soe'er|you are, |

As you see in this example, the caesura (marked by an arrow) may interrupt the foot division. Though this caesura is in the middle of the line, it could occur anywhere and there may be more than one in a line:

Too lit|tlĕ care | of this. | Take phy|sic, pomp; |

Lines may end on either stressed or unstressed syllables. Most common are those ending on stresses, which are called *masculine* endings. An unstressed syllable at the end of a line is a *feminine* ending. Often such a final syllable will be hypermetrical and was not meant to be elided:

Hĕ was |ă thing | of blood | whose ev|ery mot|*ion*
Was timed | with dy|ing cries. | Alone | he en|*ter'd*

The mor|tal gate | of the' ci|ty, which | he pain|*ted*

With shun|less des|tiny; |

In these lines from *Coriolanus*, we feel the effect of the extra last syllable "driving" us on into the next line, supporting the vigor and determination of what is being described.

When lines, like these, "run on" into each other, they are called *enjambed* lines. *Enjambed* lines are the opposite of *end-stopped* lines. Several lines may be enjambed to form a larger rhythmic unit.

Just as in prose, poetic lines form sentences, and these sentences form verse paragraphs. These are larger rhythmic patters, which we must manifest in our delivery to give the proper shaping to the development of the ideas in our speeches. These larger patterns can be analyzed just as if they were prose.

We have seen that the various levels or layers of poetic rhythm exist simultaneously, and their interaction produces a contrapuntal richness, which provides emphasis and texture. We can list these layers of rhythm from those producing the smallest patterns to those producing the largest:

1. The arrangement of stressed and unstressed syllables;
2. The division of these syllable patterns into feet and the tension between word division and foot division;
3. Variations within the basic foot pattern;
4. The placement of caesura within the line;
5. The manipulation of line-endings to form larger patterns;
6. The grouping of several lines into a verse paragraph.

PROSE RHYTHMS

A skillful writer utilizes rhythm purposefully, whether he is writing prose or poetry. Prose rhythms are usually not as heightened or formalized as those of poetry, but they operate on much the same principle of *variety in regularity*.

The basic rhythm of prose, like that of poetry, is established by the alternation of stressed and unstressed syllables as they fall into characteristic rhythmic units. While they are not identifiable by tradition or some system of nomenclature, the sensitive reader will quickly sense the "beat" underlying a prose speech. The rhythmic layers of prose we will call *cadences*, and this basic rhythm is the *syllabic cadence*.

A word of caution: *basic rhythm, in either prose or poetry is not the same thing as the tempo of the speech*. Just as waltz time can be played quickly or slowly and still be $\frac{3}{4}$ time, a passage of prose or iambic pentameter can be read with any tempo. The basic meter establishes internal relationships or *proportions* of one syllable to other syllables, while tempo is determined by the meaning, over-all patterning, and emotion.

Next in the hierarchy of cadences is the the *breath cadence*. The evolution of our written language was greatly influenced by the way we speak, and we still tend to break our sentences up into smaller units which can easily be said in one breath. These breath cadences are sometimes marked by commas (in music, the comma is still used specifically as a breath mark), but often not. Playwrights, since they are writing specifically for the human voice and not for the eye, manipulate breath cadences to guide the actor to a pattern of breathing. This breath pattern will in turn lead him to an appropriate over-all tempo, and we have already seen how the rhythm of breath is a primary factor in the generation of emotion. The sample analysis of the speech from *The Zoo Story* will deal particularly with this use of breath cadence. Note that breath cadences are also important in poetry, often coinciding with caesuras and end-stopped lines, and influence our breathing in the same way.

If the breath cadence usually expresses one phrase or sub-unit of a thought, the unit of thought which several breath cadences form can be called a *sectional* cadence, and is set off by pauses slightly stronger than the of the breath. Such pauses are usually marked by semicolons or colons.

A still larger pattern is developed by the length of sentences and independent phrases, the ends of which are marked by a strong pause symbolized by a period, question mark, or exclamation point. This is called the *terminal cadence*. In longer speeches, especially, it helps us to organize the thoughts of the speech into coherent groupings. Radical changes in the terminal cadence are usually our best indicators about changes in tempo. Terminal cadences are also of great importance in poetry as organizing factors and tempo indicators.

Finally, in extremely long speeches, there may be a *paragraph* cadence, with the end of the paragraph symbolizing a major change in thought and therefore a major pause. In most dialogue, however, the speeches by the individual characters themselves act as paragraphs. We get a good impression of the tempo of a scene by looking at the density of the printed script. A mass of long speeches suggests a different approach to tempo than, for example, the extremely short "pingpong"-like exchange of some farce.

YOUR BASIS FOR ANALYSIS

Remember that, as in the case of tone, the rhythm of speech does not determine meaning or even emotion. As you begin to analyze rhythm, you will see many possibilities and you will probably be puzzled about how to select one or another of them. Your choice must be based upon your understanding of the meaning of the line and your evaluation of the relative importance of its various elements, taking into account the demands of character, situation, and emotion as well.

Nevertheless, a detailed analysis of sound and rhythm, if it only reveals the possibilities to you (and it will usually do much more), should begin to impart to you the sense of the personality of the speaker. In our social, everyday life, we all have an intuitive and highly developed sense of the communicative value of sound and rhythm. It is what gives our speech its color and individual flavor, and is what helps us to catch implications, sarcasm, and all sorts of connotative values, which round out our daily speech and make it fully human. In any good writing, these aspects of melody have been incorporated into the structure of the lines in a carefully selected and heightened way. Through careful and informed analysis, we can unlock these inherent values of tone and rhythm, and through diligent practice and arduous technique, bring them back to life for our audiences.

SAMPLE RHYTHM ANALYSES

1. Poor na|ked wret|ches, where|soe'er | you are,

2. That bide | the pel|ting of | this pit|iless storm,

3. How shall | your house|less heads | and un|fed sides,

4. Your loop'd | and win|dow'd rag|gedness, | defend | you

5. From sea|sons such | as these? | O! I | have ta'en

6. Too lit|tle care | of this. | Take phy|sic, pomp;

7. Expose | thyself | to feel | what wret|ches feel,

8. That thou | mayst shake | the su|perflux | to them,

9. And show | the hea|vens | more | just.

KING LEAR. Examine the above sample scansion for metrical variation. Notice especially the use of spondees in the first feet of lines 1, 3, and 6. There is also a pair of spondees in the fourth feet of lines 5 and 6. The speech has a strongly emphatic quality, and the heaviness of these stresses contributes to the quietly but strongly determined compassion Lear expresses in this speech.

In line 2, we follow custom by eliding *pitiless*. The fact that we "mispronounce" the word when making the elision helps call attention to the aspect of justice it represents.

Line 4 appears to have a hypermetrical feminine ending, with the final *you* being the extra syllable. There are two reasons for this: first, the leftover beat moves us on strongly into the next line, and this is one of the two run-on lines in the speech; second, the word *you*, which appears in some form in lines 1, 3, and 4, shows Lear's concern for others. At the beginning of the play, he was self-concerned, but through his suffering he learns concern for others. His realization of his past lack of compassion is crystallized in this speech. In the first four lines, his attention is on the *poor*. In line 5, he realizes his own guilty share of things with *O! I have ta'en/ Too little care of this*. Then for the remaining lines, his attention turns again to others, those who are rich as he himself once was, and he prays that they will act as he did not.

The elision of *taken* into *ta'en* in line 5 is marked by the printer. Nevertheless, we might argue with it. There are only two run-on lines in the speech, lines 4 and 5; line 4, directly preceding, uses a hypermetrical feminine ending to move us over the line-ending and into the next one. Therefore, it might be consistent to utilize the same device in line 5 and leave *taken* as a hypermetrical feminine ending. It is further true that feminine endings usually appear in groups in Shakespeare. The decision, however, is yours and your director's. Most scholars would favor the elision. This may seem like a ridiculously small point, but crucial meanings sometimes turn on such minute detail.

The terminal cadences and placement of caesura in this speech are intriguing. The first four lines and three feet are one long and cohesive sentence. There follows the short sentence, *O! I have ta'en/ too little care of this*, which, though it is broken up by the line endings, reads as one line of iambic pentameter formed by the caesuras in lines 5 and 6. There then follows the short phrase *Take physic, pomp*, which is itself broken by a caesura. The remainder of the speech is one sentence, which flows smoothly until we come to the last line. *Heaven* could be elided to *Heav'n* (this is a common Shakespearean elision though it is difficult to pronounce) and the line could scan as regular iambic trimeter:

And show | the heavens | more just.

This seems terribly weak, however, and this shortening of this line seems to suggest that Shakespeare wanted it sustained to fill the time usually taken by a full five feet. I have therefore scanned the speech to used implied pauses as

And show | the heav|ens (–) (⌣) | more | (⌣) just. |

This results in a reading that emphasizes the concept of justice, provides a strong rhythmic finish for this crucial speech, and makes positive use of the line's irregularity. Again, however, there is no absolute rule about such matters.

Accepting the scansion, we see a beautiful shaping of the whole speech. Since caesuras give the effect, in reading, of a "false" line ending, and strong run-on lines obscure actual line endings, we could print and read the speech like this:

Poor naked wretches,

Wheresoe'er you are,

That bide the pelting of this pitless storm,

How shall your houseless heads and unfed sides,

Your loop'd and window'd raggedness,

defend you from seasons such as these?

O!

I have ta'en too little care of this.

Take physic,

pomp;

Expose thyself to feel what wretches feel,

That thou mayst shake the superflux to them,

And show the heavens

more

just.

As it is printed here each line represents a breath cadence. Read it aloud, taking a breath for each line and see what effect this has on your tempo, and what emotion begins to result. Do you see which ideas and feelings are emphasized by this shaping of the whole?

THE ZOO STORY. As in the speech from *King Lear*, cadences play a crucial role in shaping here. The syllabic cadence is heavily stressed, since the preponderance of words are of one syllable. The effect is emphatic. The hard consonant and fricative sounds combine with this rhythm to produce a stacatto effect, like sharp tapping on a snare drum. As the speech progresses, however, the beat and tones change, deepen, and quicken, until they are like a prolonged tympani roll.

The breath cadence is probably the most crucial rhythmic level in this speech. The pauses, which Albee has indicated by three dots, form a pattern of breath reminiscent of orgasm, beginning short and fragmentary, lengthening and swelling, reaching a prolonged climax in lines 18-20, and then dying away in a few final gasps, finishing with a heavy sigh. The use of capital letters as volume and emphasis markings support this pattern. Imagine the speech printed *as if it were modern poetry*. Where would you break the lines? Try marking the breath cadences and imagine the speech printed the way the speech from *Lear* is printed above. Read it aloud as if each breath cadence were a line of poetry, and see what tempos result.

The terminal cadence supports this pattern also. If you mark the major punctuation, a pattern like this emerges:

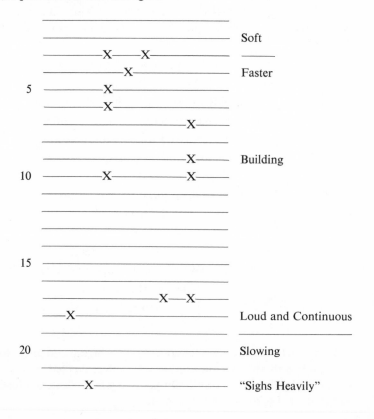

Just as in the speech from *King Lear*, certain ideas are emphasized by being isolated as short units surrounded by longer cadences. The long, continuous terminal cadence, which begins in line 10, runs until the semicolon in line 17, and is followed by the two words, *with God*. The question of God, then, is the culmination of Jerry's verbal searching during the first part of the speech. Once he has crystallized his feelings in this concept, the full outburst, the section in capital letters, is unleashed. Then, his energy spent, he says *"with God who, I'm told, turned his back on the whole thing some time ago. . . ,"* he returns to his starting point, *people*.

Exercise 39: Rhythm Polarization

Since the speech you have chosen for the polarization exercises is highly poetic, scan it very carefully. Then analyze its various rhythmic levels. Typing several carbon copies of the speech will enable you to use markings, colored pencils, and so on, to help visualize the rhythmic patterning. Now, *without using the actual words of the original:*

1. Using dance or marching movements, hand clapping or other devices, perform the speech to exaggerate the *basic* rhythmic pattern. Then do it again, emphasizing as many of the *variations* as you can. Finally, do a full movement expression of what you consider the important *basic* rhythmic qualities of the speech, without trying to recreate every specific rhythm.
2. Now do this basic rhythmic expression of the scene, allowing the movement to produce noises that are the natural outgrowth of the body's activity. Does your vocal sound come freely, or have you not yet integrated vocal activity with all the other forms of muscular activity? How much of the meaning and emotion of the original is retained, or extended, in this performance?

In the course of these polarizations, have you discovered inflectional patterns, pitch ranges, perhaps even postures, types of walking and movement, or other physical qualities, which have helped create a full experience of the speech for your whole body? If you haven't, you are probably failing to analyze carefully enough or, more likely, failing to involve your muscles fully in the polarization exercises. Has part of your body been unavailable during the exercises? Have you avoided the fullest possible movement, with the excuse that it isn't "real" or "believable," or that you just "don't know what kinds of movement to use?" Remember that these are *training exercises*, not performance or even rehearsal techniques. The aim is to create a full, organic experience *for yourself*, based upon the important qualities of text, which you have identified through careful analysis. As such, the completeness and commitment of your movement and noises is far more important than their "correctness" in terms of a performance. Don't evade the experience; move! make noise!

Analyzing
the Speech:
Vocal Melody

There is a story about the famous Italian actress, Eleanora Duse, who moved a New York audience to tears by reading the Manhattan telephone book in Italian. Since the audience didn't understand Italian, her speech was communicative strictly as gesture, as a *vocal melody*.

Any good actor develops great expressiveness in the use of the sound of speech, apart from the dictionary meaning of those sounds as words. This applies not only to moans and sighs and other noises we make that are not words, but to the sounds that make up words themselves. What guides us in our use of vocal melody—our own feelings, as in the story above?

Usually, as actors, we are not speaking meaningless sounds or words of our own invention, but words that have been chosen and arranged by a playwright. Any good playwright has selected these words, not only because of what they mean (for there are often many words that could produce roughly the same meaning), but also because of the way they *sound*. Our use of vocal melody on the stage should be controlled by the author's use of it in his text.

THE VOCO-SENSORY THEORY

There have been attempts to develop systems that will "de-code" vocal melody and attach certain emotional meanings to certain sounds. The most famous of these was the *Roback Voco-Sensory Theory*. Experimental subjects were asked to tell which of several three-letter nonsense syllables, like *mil* and *mal*, made them think of larger or smaller objects. As you probably guessed, *mal* seemed "bigger" than *mil*. The theory explains this by pointing out that the physical act of saying *mal* requires opening the mouth more than does saying *mil*. The "big" space in the mouth causes the sensation of bigness associated with *mal*, while the reverse is true for *mil*. The theory goes on to suggest that much of language was formed by this sort of translation of physical sensations into appropriate sounds, hence the name *voco-sensory* theory. "Rough" words *sound* rough, "smooth" words *sound* smooth, for example. Indeed, they often do, just as *rushing* rushes, *explode* explodes, and so on.

This is an interesting view of language for the actor, since it provides a relationship between physical sensation and the meanings of words. However, it has become obsolete, since many words do *not* seem to relate to physical sensations, and because of the many exceptions to the rule. *Small* is made of "big" sounds, while *big* is "small." Let us suggest that the physical sensations of words are often more important to their *connotation* than to their *denotation*.

If we examine a sentence like "the ghost wind howled a scream," we can see how many sensations appropriate to the mood are contained in the windiness of *wind*, the howling of *howled*, and the scream of *scream*. We can also see that the organ-like open vowel tones of *ghost* and *howled* alternate with the thin sounds of *wind* and *scream*, providing an ebb and flow, a rising and falling like the "ghost wind" itself. But all these qualities of the sentence's melody can be analyzed only *after* we have understood its meaning and emotional intention. With exactly the same sounds, in the same arrangement, we can also say, "the Post-Six Bowling Team."

Although the voco-sensory theory has fallen into disfavor, we can still learn a great deal from it. It awakens us to the importance of speech melody as it provides a physical manifestation of appropriate connotations. A good playwright will have selected words whose sounds can be useful to us in supporting the meaning and emotional tone of our speech. As long as we remember that meaning is not *determined* by sound, but is *supported* by it, we will be able to find the physical aspects of pronouncing the speech that will generate and communicate appropriate emotions.

ONOMATOPOEIA AND ALLITERATION

There are a few technical terms we should learn to describe the patterning of sounds in our speeches, remembering that our *use* of these patterns is the important thing. The first is *onomatopoeia*. This refers to words whose sound resembles the thing they describe. Even if there is no specific use of onomatopoeia, a good writer will have supplied us with sounds that we can emphasize to heighten the effect of a line. When Juliet says "Gallop apace, you fiery-footed steeds," we recognize that *gallop* can be pronounced so as to sound like a horse galloping, and is onomatopoeic. But *fiery*, although there is no particular sound connected with fieriness, lends itself to being spoken in a fiery manner. The quick explosion of air from between our lips on the *fi* sound can be the sort of aggressive, bold attack we connect with fieriness.

Notice how the poet has reinforced the onomatopoeia of *gallop* by repeating the key sounds in other words: "Gallo*p* a*p*ace" not only sounds like galloping, but because the sounds are repeated in close proximity and the rhythm is arranged to move quickly, it sounds like *fast* galloping, which is exactly appropriate to the sense of the line. Likewise, the repetition of the *f* sound in "*f*iery-*f*ooted" helps reinforce the effect of fieriness, and also relates fieriness to the feet of the horses, thus referring us back to a quality of their galloping.

This repetition of similar initial sounds of words in close juxtaposition is called *alliteration*. We can use the term broadly to refer to all closely repeated sounds that form melodic patterns, being equally interested in repeated vowel and consonant sounds whether they occur as *initial* sounds or *within* the words. As in the case of onomatopoeia, the actor should be liberal in his application of this principle.

Though alliteration formally applies to sounds which are quite close together, we will also be interested in types of sounds that recur within a speech or even within a role. While individual cases of alliteration or onomatopoeia can be used for emphasis of particular points, the over-all patterning of sounds on a larger scale produces an effect that good writers will use to help distinguish one role from another, one mood from another, or the changing of emotional states within a role.

You might find, for example, that the sounds of your speeches make a particular pitch range and inflectional pattern more comfortable than others, and that this pitch and pattern will be psychologically and physically appropriate to your role. The melody of our speeches suggests vocal qualities of delivery, which in turn suggest aspects of characterization.

MELODY AND CHARACTERIZATION

We cannot, unfortunately, go into an intensive study of the effect of age and social background on voice, or of dialects and the other complexities of vocal characterization. Such an advanced study demands considerable basic skill. But even on a beginning level, the effect of voice on total characterization is apparent.

One of the most important functions of speech-melody is that it serves as a link between the words of our written text and our total physical performance. Any skillful playwright has incorporated in the words of his play a wealth of vocal actions, which can lead the sensitive actor to a full involvement with his character. Stanislavski, in *Building a Character*, put it this way:

> Letters, syllables, words—these are the musical notes of speech, out of which we fashion measures, arias, whole symphonies. There is good reason

to describe beautiful speech as musical. . . . Even if we do not understand the meaning of words, their sounds effect us through their tempo-rhythms. . . . There is an indissoluble interdependence, interaction and bond between tempo-rhythms. . . . The correctly established tempo-rhythm of a role, can of itself, intuitively (on occasion automatically) take hold of the feelings of an actor and arouse in him a true sense of living his part.[28]

SYNTHESIZING MELODY IN PERFORMANCE

When we fully revitalize the melody of a speech, we find that the sounds help to make the feelings and meaning more vivid and more immediate. We should not merely "act out" the sounds, but treat them as "sound effects," which are an integral part of the speech's meaning. We usually see dance accompanied by music; the physical aspects of our stage performance are likewise accompanied by the melody of speech. But in a great dance, the music doesn't simply accompany; the movements and music have been synthesized into an indivisible expressive whole. Such is the case of the great stage performance as well.

SAMPLE MELODY ANALYSES

KING LEAR. The melody of poetry is carefully patterned, and it is often useful to chart graphically the recurrent sounds, by underlining, coloring, or some other device.

In line 1, the falling vowel sound of *Poor* followed by the hard, almost cruel sound of *naked* set the mood. These sounds, of course, are not *of themselves* hard or soft, but can be *used* to physicalize the meaning of each word. The condensed quality of poetry makes it necessary to realize fully each word. As you say *Poor*, the full weight of poverty and all that it means must be present. *Naked* must likewise be delivered with a vivid sense of nakedness. The pronouncing of these words demands certain vocal and physical gestures, which must be full enough to achieve the appropriate intensity of meaning and feeling.

Wretches is a somewhat onomatopoeic word; its sound is bitter and regurgitative as in "retching." *Wretches, wheresoe'er* is alliteration of the *w* sounds, extending the effect. *Wheresoe'er you are* is a triple repetition of *r* sounds.

---

[28] From *An Actor's Handbook* by Stanislavski, edited and translated by Elizabeth Reynolds Hapgood. Copyright © 1936, 1961, 1963 by Elizabeth Reynolds Hapgood. Used with the permission of the publishers, Theatre Arts Books, New York.

In line 2, *bide*, *pelting*, and *pitiless* alliterate, tying these three aspects of the condition of the poor together. *Pelting* is onomatopoeic, and the physical and vocal gestures required to pronounce it peltingly carry a sense of physical cruelty over to *pitiless* which contains roughly the same sounds, turning it into an especially ruthless and active lack of compassion and morality. Try continuing the analysis yourself for lines 3-6.

In line 7, *Expose* is a sound that begins small and opens, "exposing" the mouth, and this quality can be extended to our whole body and attitude, so that Lear does physically expose himself here *to feel what wretches feel*, the alliteration emphasizing the important point *to feel*, to have compassion, to *not* be pitiless. Lear calls this speech a *prayer* earlier, and a gesture of exposure from a prayerful attitude might be to throw the arms open into a pose reminiscent of the crucifixion, the pose of another man who exposed himself *to feel what wretches feel*.

The thought in lines 8 and 9 is emphasized by the balancing of the *sh* sounds in *shake* and *show*. Other qualities of these lines were discussed earlier.

THE ZOO STORY. At the beginning of the speech, the sounds are clipped and mostly consonant, emphasizing the halting quality of Jerry's thought here. But as the speech progresses and his associations begin to pour out, the sounds likewise begin to elongate, until line 18 and 19 are one prolonged tonal outcry.

There are strong onomatopoeic words in the latter half of the speech, and their qualities reflect the quality of Jerry's emotion: *bleeding*, *hard*, *oily-wet*, *wisp*, *vomiting*, *crying*, *fury*, *howling*, and so on. There is a surprising amount of alliteration as well, *wisp of smoke*, *pornographic playing*, *pretty little ladies aren't pretty little ladies*, *making money*, *COLORED QUEEN . . . KIMONO . . . PLUCKS*.

As we noted earlier, the description of Jerry's world is a strong theme in this speech. The kinds of sounds we have listed, and the gestures they demand, should be used to make Jerry's response to that world vivid, as well as making that world itself, with its illusions (*wisps of smoke; pretty little ladies aren't...*), its pain (*vomiting*, *crying*, *fury*, *howling*), and its futile efforts at meaningful contact (*pornographic playing*, *COLORED QUEEN*) as real to us as possible.

Exercise 40: Melody Polarization

Using the speech you have selected for all the polarization exercises, analyze it for its patterning of sound, then:

1. Recite it in monotone. Feel your impulse to break out of the monotone into melody. Where is this impulse the strongest?
2. Sing it as if it were pure music. Forget that the sounds have any verbal

meaning; invent a melody that stresses the sounds you have decided are most important.

3. Now repeat your rhythm polarization, but replace the "accidental" sounds that grew spontaneously from your muscular activity then with the specific sound patterns (not necessarily all the actual words) that you think are of basic significance in the speech. What do you discover about the interrelationship of sound, rhythm, and muscular activity? Retain any words of the original which are of special sound value, but treat them as pure *sound* rather than for their meaning as words.

LESSON 11

Analyzing
the Speech:
Imagery and
Figurative
Language

The skillful playwright gets an extra measure of expressiveness from his language by utilizing the sensory potential of certain words, and arranging words in special combinations which produce heightened meanings. In this way words can be *used* not only to communicate meaning and connotated feelings, but to create sensations and insights that revitalize our awareness of reality. The creation of sensation by words is *imagery*, and heightened meaning achieved by special combinations of words is *figurative language*.

SENSE IMAGERY

Imagery is often subtle or even hidden beneath the surface of seemingly ordinary speech. For this reason, we cannot trust to intuition, but must carefully analyze and internalize the imagery of our speeches. In its most literal sense, "imagery" refers to "something imagined," the painting of word-pictures. But the general category of imagery encompasses many more types of images than just "word-painting." Images can appeal to *any* of our senses. This speech from Shakespeare's *Antony and Cleopatra* describes Cleopatra's royal barge sailing down the Nile in the night, and it is filled with imagery:

> The barge she sat in, like a burnish'd throne,
> Burn'd on the water. The poop was beaten gold;
> Purple the sails, and so perfumed that
> The winds were love-sick with them; the oars were silver,
> Which to the tune of flutes kept stroke, and made
> The water which they beat to follow faster,

As amorous of their strokes. For her own person,
It beggar'd all description. She did lie
In her pavilion, cloth-of-gold, of tissue,
O'erpicturing that Venus where we see
The fancy out-work nature. On each side of her
Stood pretty dimpled boys, like smiling Cupids,
With divers-colour'd fans, whose wind did seem
To glow the delicate cheeks which they did cool,
And what they undid did.

The picture of the barge drawn by these words is so vivid that we can "see" it in the mind's eye. This "word-painting" aspect of the speech is called *visual imagery*. But we can find examples of almost every other type of sense imagery in this speech as well. The silver oars "which to the tune of flutes kept stroke," appeals to our hearing and is an *aural* image. The "perfumed sails which made the winds love-sick" appeals to our sense of smell and is an *olfactory* image. The humorous reference to the water chasing the oars, as if the oars' strokes were lovers' caresses, and the smoothness of the fabric of Cleopatra's pavilion awaken our sense of touch and texture, and are *tactile* imagery. The cooling breeze of the fans and the flowing warmth of Cleopatra's cheeks are contrasted *thermal* images. If only Cleopatra were (as she might well have been) dining upon some exotic delicacy, we might have been treated to some tasty *gustatory* imagery.

Throughout the description of the barge, we have a sense of its slow, gliding movement on the water, of the softly billowing sails, of the rhythmic stroking of the oars. Such senses of movement and physical states are categorized in two types of imagery. *Kinetic* imagery refers to our sense of actual movement (like the barge's sailing). *Kinesthetic* imagery refers to our sense of physical states that do not necessarily involve movement, such as our sense of Cleopatra's relaxation upon her cushions.

Kinesthetic imagery often serves as a "background," a general physical state that underlies other sensations. If, for example, we put ourselves completely in the place of the speaker here and attempt to rejuvenate all his original responses, we would have to be aware of the feeling of the openness of the night air stretching out over the dark water, and the cool breeze upon our face. This generalized kinesthetic response helps us to recreate a scene as vividly as possible by imaginatively "putting us in the picture."

The vividness of our response to images, our ability to recreate the sensations as if they were happening for the first time, is the crucial factor in communicating the images to the audience. By fully physicalizing our own response, we are in the best position to inspire a similar response in the audience. In this way we do not simply ask our audience to respond to us: we have helped them to visualize and respond to the scene for themselves.

SAMPLE IMAGERY ANALYSES

KING LEAR. The context of this speech gives us a clear idea of its kinesthetic background—Lear using a lull in the storm to adopt a prayerful attitude. Notice how the words that melody and rhythm have already emphasized are also rich in images. The speech is about the poor, and the visual images make the poor vivid to the mind's eye: *naked wretches, houseless heads, unfed sides,* and so on, and the periodic syntax of the first four lines causes these images to "fund" into a single impact. As you examine each visual image, you find that they also have strong kinesthetic content: *naked, houseless, unfed,* and so on. Lear not only makes us *see* the poor, he makes us *feel* what it is to be poor as well, as he himself does at this moment. Supporting this is the strong tactile image, the *pelting* of the storm. Continue the analysis yourself, recognizing each of the many sensations contained in the speech and identifying the way each supports and heightens meaning.

THE ZOO STORY. This speech is filled with a host of images. The visual images are preponderant and, again, the sound, rhythm, and our diction study have already picked out the key ones. As in Lear's prayer, Albee has provided a clear kinesthetic context for the speech, both in the situation and in the stage directions. Jerry, growing more and more tense, is heading for an explosion; the climax of this speech is one of the minor climaxes leading up to his death.

Besides the obvious visual images, there are a good many other types. The touch of things seems important to Jerry, and most of the visual images have a tactile impact as well. Textures are contrasted in *oily-wet* and *wisp of smoke.* The sequence of kinesthetic and partly kinetic images—*vomiting, crying, fury, making money with your body, act of love, howling, WEARS A KIMONO, PLUCKS HIS EYEBROWS, CRIES WITH DETERMINATION, turned his back*—has already been discussed as diction, but here the uniquely physical imagistic content makes us aware of a sequential development that relates to Jerry's physical responses to his world.

In both these speeches, the physical vividness of images supports meaning and emotion. These speeches also demonstrate how important the interaction of types of images is, and how a single word often has several imagistic values.

Exercise 41: Imagery Polarization

Again perform a word-dance of your speech in slow motion, but this time exaggerate in your physical responses the sensory impact of each image.

Treat each image individually and fully explore it, attempting to "re-live" the sensation of each. Then speed your dance up to normal tempo, and concentrate on the flow of your physical responses to the images. How does this sensory content relate to the meaning and emotion of the speech? *Be sure to involve the articulation of the words directly in your physical actions in all the remaining exercises.*

FIGURATIVE LANGUAGE

Also called "figures of speech," *figurative* language is contrasted with *literal* language. When we speak *literally*, words can be taken at their face value. But when we speak *figuratively*, we combine words (place them into a *configuration*) to make them express more than their face value, producing new units of meaning and reference. We will divide the figures of speech into three categories: 1) *sound* figures, which depend upon the patterning of sounds, and *diction* figures, which require the selection and manipulation of specific word meanings; 2) *structural* figures, which are products of syntax, and 3) *types of metaphor*, which combine disparate elements to create new meanings.

1. SOUND AND DICTION FIGURES. You are already familiar with several figures of speech. The sound figures, for example, are alliteration and onomatopoeia. You also know two of the diction figures, puns and archaisms. Another common diction figure is *allusion*, a brief reference to a person, place, or thing, which the writer assumes will be known to the audience, who will then "fill in" the reference from their own knowledge. When Juliet, looking at the sky, says "Gallop apace, you fiery footed steeds," Shakespeare assumes that the audience will know that she is alluding to the chariot of Apollo, which, according to myth, carries the sun across the heavens. Since she wants Apollo's horses to hurry, we understand that she wants night to fall as soon as possible, because then Romeo will come. The last of the diction figures we will cover is *hyperbole*, the use of conscious exaggeration for either comic or serious effect. Lear says, "Had I your tongues and eyes I'd use 'em so heaven's vault should crack," which is an exaggeration expressive of the magnitude of his grief.

2. STRUCTURAL FIGURES. Structural figures achieve their meaning by arranging elements of a line or speech so that they are contrasted or compared. These figures are helpful in suggesting line readings, since we must emphasize the comparisons being made through our use of pitch and emphasis. Even physical gesture will be involved in a full response to the shaping of structural figures.

We have already met one structural figure in the last line of the description of Cleopatra's barge. Boys are standing beside Cleopatra fanning her, and the wind from the fans "did seem to glow the delicate cheeks which they did cool,/

And what they *undid did.*" This is a *paradox*, a seemingly impossible combination of words which turns out to have a coherent meaning. In this case, the wind from the fans, instead of cooling Cleopatra, acts like a bellows on a fire, causing her to glow like a burning ember. Since they are trying to "undo" her heat but in fact they make her hotter, we can say that "what they undid" they "did." This is a marvelous way of expressing the torrid quality of the sensuous Cleopatra.

A very important structural figure for the actor, and one of Shakespeare's favorite devices, is *antithesis*, which places two halves of a line or speech in contrast. The two sections will have a similar syntax, but different meanings. In this speech from *Romeo and Juliet*, Juliet has just learned that Romeo has killed her cousin Tybalt in a fight. Naturally, she is torn between her love for Romeo and abhorrence of what he has done. This ambivalence manifests itself in a series of antitheses:

> O *serpent heart*, hid with a *flowering face*!
> Did ever *dragon* keep so *fair* a cave?
> *Beautiful tyrant! fiend angelical!*
> *Dove-feathered raven! Wolvish-ravening lamb!*
> *Despised substance* of *divinest show!*
> *Just opposite* to what thou *justly seem'st,*
> A *damned saint,* an *honorable villain*!

The compared elements in each line are in italics; as you read them aloud, you will find yourself naturally physicalizing this balanced structure in inflection, pitch, gesture, and so on.

Notice the combination of words with opposite meanings and connotations in a single phrase, like *fiend angelical* and *Dove-feathered raven*. This direct juxtaposing of opposite sensations or meanings is called *oxymoron*. If we look at the structure of one of the lines using both these devices, we see

Beautiful tyrant!   fiend angelical!
⤿oxymoron⤾   ⤿oxymoron⤾

a pattern demanding the utmost skill from the actor in the use of inflection, emphasis, pitch, and supportive gesture.

3. VARIETIES OF METAPHOR. This is the broadest and most complex category of figurative language. While a *metaphor* is a certain kind of figure of speech, the metaphorical *process* or *principle* is common to a good many related figures. All types of metaphor have one thing in common: they take disparate things or ideas, and "combine" them in order to reveal a new meaning. Imagine the superimposition of two images in a movie; the two images combine to make a new image with a meaning of its own, a meaning that transcends the individual meanings of the two previously separate

images. In this same way, metaphorical combinations of words crystallize a wealth of meaning in a single image.

When we say *he's a rat*, we have taken two different kinds of things and put them together, at least verbally, in such a way as to make them seem identical. *He* (man) is one kind of thing; *rat* is another kind. *He is a rat* implies by its construction that man and rat are identical. It is obvious that man and rat are not identical in *all* ways, so the metaphor refers only to certain qualities that might be shared by both. "Man" and "rat" may share qualities like cowardice, dirtiness, wile, meanness, and so on. We project these qualities of rat-ness upon the object of our metaphor. The object of the metaphor is called the *tenor*; the metaphorical word (here, *rat*) is the *vehicle*.

We value metaphor because it can achieve new and often startling meanings through the combination of otherwise familiar words. The more startling the combination, the greater the insight it may give us, and the best metaphors combine extremely dissimilar ideas. In *Othello*, Iago sums up his moral code with a tremendous metaphor, which combines the lowliest of real and perishable objects with the highest of abstract concepts; "Virtue? A fig!" Our delivery should make the surprise of the combination vivid, by giving each of the two words its full individual value, thereby heightening their dissimilarity rather than diminishing it. Besides *pure* metaphor, in which dissimilar things are used as if they were *identical*, there are several more moderate forms of metaphor.

The mildest form of metaphor is *simile*. Here the elements are not directly combined, but only compared, shown to be *similar*, not *identical*. The comparison is usually expressed by a word such as "like" or "as." In the Cleopatra scene, the "pretty dimpled boys," who fan the Queen are compared to mythological figures, "like smiling Cupids." In paintings of Venus, goddess of love, cupids were often shown hovering near her. The picture of Cleopatra lying on her pillows with cupids about her is a simile combined with an allusion referring to Cleopatra's superhuman beauty.

Several other types of metaphors have been given their own names. *Personification* occurs when an inanimate object or abstract idea is described as if it were alive, as when Macbeth describes his own greed as, "vaulting ambition, which o'erleaps itself . . .". If the abstract or inanimate thing is not merely described, but is spoken to as if it were alive rather than merely being described, we have *apostrophe*. Edmund, in *King Lear* apostrophizes, "Nature, thou art my goddess!"

When a part of something is mentioned as if it were the whole, it is *synecdoche*, as when Juliet calls Romeo a *serpent heart*. When one thing is used to refer to something else with which it is closely associated, as when we say "the crown" when we mean "the position of king," it is *metonomy*.

4. CLUSTERING OF IMAGES AND FIGURES OF SPEECH. Figures of speech and images form an important element of a play's whole structure

when they appear in clusters, or when they recur throughout a role or play as *motifs*, such as the recurrent references to nature in various forms in *King Lear*, or the recurring references to food and eating and drinking in *The Zoo Story*. Such clusters and motifs can be indications of dominant attitudes in a character, or of important thematic content in a role. Often these motifs will not simply recur, but will change and develop within a play, providing concrete "touchstones" for the actor as his character develops. In *Lear*, for example, Lear's references at the beginning of the play are ornate allusions to pagan gods, and his images are of regal splendor. During his madness, his images become bestial, sexual, and scatalogical. By the end of the play they are simple and human; he no longer speaks of "Hecate" and "Juno" but simply of "God." He no longer speaks of himself as a "dragon and his wrath" but as a "fond, foolish, old man." These developing images and figurative motifs, when carefully examined and physicalized by the actor, help him to manifest many important changes in his character.

SAMPLE ANALYSES OF FIGURATIVE LANGUAGE

KING LEAR. The entire speech is an apostrophe to the *poor* (11. 1-5) and to the *rich* (11. 6-9). In apostrophe, we must direct our concentration to the imagined object of our speech, here visualizing clearly, but in a generalized way, the lowly poor, then the exalted rich. This gives the speech two sections, separated by Lear's awareness of himself in lines 5 and 6, and this suggests to the actor a physical change to delineate the sections.

The sound and diction figures have already been mentioned, except for what could be considered a hyperbole in the last line—Lear's characteristic scope of thought in showing the heavens themselves *more just. Houseless heads and unfed sides* in line 3, since they refer not just to "heads" and "sides" but to the whole persons, are synecdoches, which suggest a strongly physical response. The use of *pomp* in line 6, since it refers not just to the regal splendor of the rich but to the rich themselves, is a metonymy.

THE ZOO STORY. The speech revolves around the central metaphor in lines 18-20. Earlier there are two "submerged" metaphors. In line 9, the toilet paper is a mirror; the usual mirror is one in which we see our face, where the world enters us in breathing and eating. Toilet paper is a mirror of the orifice through which the world leaves us, as excrement and occasionally, appropriately to Jerry's torment, as blood.

The *strongbox . . . WITHOUT A LOCK* in lines 14-15 is a metaphor for accessibility, for the possibility of being "open," just as the woman's *CLOSED DOOR* is an antithetical image. Also a strongbox that cannot be locked is useless, unable, like Jerry, to fulfill the purpose for which it was created.

Finally, the central metaphor is that *GOD* is *A COLORED QUEEN* and *A WOMAN WHO CRIES*. God, the fulfillment of all human aspirations, of all possibilities of goodness and perfection, is, for Jerry, the choice between illusory, perverted sexual relationships on the one hand, and complete isolation and determined sorrow on the other.

These are the qualities revealed by the metaphor, and as in manifesting any figure of speech in our performance, the revealed qualities communicated by the structure of the figure provide rich physical suggestions to the responsive actor.

Exercise 42: Figurative Language Polarization

Find ways to physicalize each figure of speech in your selection, so as to communicate its structure and its meaning to your audience. Don't be tied to a realistic delivery; *your aim is to make the figurative language as literal as possible in your performance*, to "release" the wealth of meaning that has been condensed in each figure of speech. Again, remember to involve the physical act of articulating the words of the speech directly in your overall activity. Do *not* separate the words and the actions, but emphasize their inter-relationship. The audience should *hear* the effect of your actions on your voice, and *see* the effect of your voice on your actions.

Play Structure
and Action

So far we have been analyzing the words that are the "building blocks" of the play. Now we are ready to examine the larger pattern of experience they form.

The largest pattern we can perceive in a play is the pattern of its over-all shape, the manner in which all the elements that make up the play have been combined into an artistically unified whole. This quality of artistic unity, this over-all patterning, we will call the play's structure or *organization*.

Although many works of art of the same generic type (for example, classical tragedy, Restoration comedy, and so on) share similar structural conventions, every successful work of art also has its own unique structural identity. The actor, his director, the designers, the technicians, all strive to contribute to a fulfillment of the play's structural unity in an appropriately unified stage production. Therefore, a clear view of the whole and a clear sense of how your character contributes to the whole must be the foundation of your creation.

ACTION AND STRUCTURE

The arts are distinguished from each other by the materials they use. Any organization of sounds may be music; any organization of words may be literature; any organization of line, mass, and color on a ground may be painting or other graphic art, and so on. The material that distinguishes drama is *human action*; therefore, any organization of human actions may be drama.

Human action is the foundation of all drama. We must remember, though, that *action*, as we use the term, does not refer exclusively to *events*; it is also the tension that precedes an event, or even tension that might potentially *become* an event. There are many contemporary plays with no "events" at all in the traditional sense (Beckett's *Waiting for Godot*, Pinter's *The Dumbwaiter*, Ionesco's *Victims of Duty*, to name a few), and yet these plays are rich in the dynamic tensions that provide a strong sense of dramatic *action*.

Because of the nature of the material of drama then, *a play's structural unity depends on how its human action has been organized* and how all the other elements of the play (the characters, their thoughts and feelings, the way in which they express themselves, and all which the audience hears and sees) contribute to that organization, or *plot*.

The organization of a play's plot may be based upon several principles. Oscar Brockett has suggested three in his *The Theatre: An Introduction*:

> Traditionally, the dominant organizational principle has been the *cause-to-effect* arrangement of incidents. Using this method, the playwright sets up in the opening scenes all of the necessary conditions—the situation, the desires and motivations of the characters—out of which the later events develop. The goals of one character come into conflict with those of another, or two conflicting desires within the same character may lead to a crisis. Attempts to surmount the obstacles make up the substance of the play, each scene growing logically out of those which have preceded it.
>
> Less often, a dramatist uses a *character* as the principal source of unity. In this case, the incidents are held together primarily because they center around one person. Such a play may dramatize the life of an historical figure, or it may show a character's responses to a series of experiences. This kind of organization may be seen in such plays as Christopher Marlowe's *Doctor Faustus* and *Tamburlaine*.
>
> A playwright may organize his material around a *basic idea*, with the scenes linked largely because they illustrate aspects of a larger theme or argument. This type of organization is used frequently by modern playwrights, especially those of the Expressionist, Epic, and Absurdist movements.[29]

Of course, most plays use all three of these organizational principles to a greater or lesser degree. The last, organization around a *basic idea*, has become increasingly important. This basic idea may be *social* or *political*, as in Brecht's *Good Woman of Setzuan* or Shaw's *Major Barbara*, or *philosophical*, as in Camus' *Caligula* or Sartre's *No Exit*. It may be *moral*, an examination of the values of a society or of human relationships, as in Miller's *Death of a Salesman*, Albee's *American Dream*, or Van Itallie's *America Hurrah*.

ACTION AND MEANING

We will call the specific underlying idea of a play, whether it is the *main* organizing principle or not, the *theme* of the play. A play's *thematic content* is simply what the playwright was trying to say. This can take many forms.

For example, the underlying premise of the action or theme of Brecht's

---

[29] Oscar G. Brockett, *The Theatre: An Introduction* 2nd ed. (New York: Holt, Rinehart and Winston, Inc.: 1969), p. 29.

Mother Courage is the effect of the need for expediency, the need to "get along" by "doing business," especially in war, upon the human character. In Ibsen's *An Enemy of the People*, the central theme is that one man's conscience may be more important than the will of the majority, because the truth is not always determined by majority vote. These are themes in the traditional sense of "message" or *thesis*.

But a *theme* is not always a *thesis*, since not all plays have a "message." A theme, as the underlying premise of the plot of a play, may simply be a situation; the typical Restoration Comedy, for example, is based upon the "sex chase" of boy-wants-girl, girl-wants-boy, and the entire play is motivated by this premise. In many modern plays, the theme may be only a mood or anxiety; the underlying premise of the plot of *Waiting for Godot* is, appropriately, *waiting*, without the possibility of action or knowledge beyond the necessity to wait.

A play may have more than one basic theme, though a director will usually focus his interpretation on one. We have already pointed out that *King Lear* could be done as a play about kingship, about the generation gap, about justice, about the development of humanism, as an allegory of judgment day, and so on.

With the help of the director, the creative ensemble must agree on a view of the theme or themes of the play and see how each element of the play contributes to it.

One word of caution: The meaning of a play cannot be stated simply. When we discussed the themes of several plays above, we were only stating in oversimplified terms one of the aspects of each play's structure. The true meaning of the play lives only in the complete *experiencing* of it as a theatrical event. This experience is demanded by the *dynamic* nature of plays, and the dynamic nature of plays is produced by the *tensions* that produce *actions*. These tensions are usually (but not always) produced by the interaction of characters in a situation of *conflict*.

The nature of a play's conflict is related to the play's thematic content: A Shaw play may achieve its sense of conflict through the interplay of *ideas* represented by various characters; a Beckett play may use the attempts of the characters to cope with their *situation* as the basic conflict; in an O'Neill play, the conflict may arise from the *psychology* of the characters themselves. Whatever its source, the play's conflict is the working out in dramatic action of the thematic content of the play.

A play, then, is a meaningful organization of human action, usually related to a conflict, character, or theme, or any combination of these.

ACTION AND CHARACTER

This dramatic action, and the conflict or theme related to it, cannot exist without *characters* who perform the actions. A character may not necessarily *cause* an action, any more than a pendulum causes itself to swing, but he will always serve as a "vehicle" or *agent* for the action in which he is involved. In this way, character is the *material* out of which action is made, and the demands of the action determine the *form* the character will take.

The way the character has been formed by the playwright is largely determined by this fact. *Characters are constructed so that they can believably serve as agents for, and sometimes even seem to cause, the action of their play.* We can call this the *dramatic purpose* of the character.

This idea of *purpose* is of primary importance. Very often actors approach their characters so personally that they begin to forget the larger purpose for which that character was created. A character, as an element of a larger action, has an over-all dramatic function related to the plot of his play. He may serve as a "foil," frustrating the intentions of another character; he may be the spokesman for one of several conflicting points of view; he may simply serve to provide some essential information, like the classical messenger, and not be directly involved in the action himself; he may be a *raisonneur* who acts as the playwright's spokesman. There is almost no limit to the possible varieties of dramatic purpose—and the true life of a character is derived *only* from fulfillment of this purpose.

No matter how "alive" a portrayal may be at any given moment, if all the moments do not "add up" to fulfill the character's dramatic purpose, the actor has failed as an interpreter (however well he may have succeeded as an impersonator). In fact, the entire play is bound to fail in this case, since a play, like any mechanism, "works" only when every part has performed its job in its proper relationship with every other part. The ultimate expression of a character's dramatic purpose must live as *specific actions* contributing to the entire experience of the play.

There is an old maxim that the bad playwright *tells* you a man is a villain, while the good playwright *shows* him kicking a dog. You cannot simply go on stage and "be" a villain; you must *do* something villainous. The dynamic nature of theatre is such that you must achieve and fulfill your dramatic purpose through *activity*. Otherwise, the audience might as well stay home and read a synopsis of the play. But this action must also be a meaningful expression of dramatic purpose. Your understanding of the dramatic purpose of the character will help you to achieve a more specific and meaningful scene, while the force of the character's action will provide a vital and moving one.

ANALYZING CHARACTER ACTION

A "character action" is anything that a character does or tries to do (the attempt to do something is itself an action), and it may also be a *reaction* the character has to someone else's action or to an event or situation. In fact, *reaction* is usually more important than action. The dictum that "acting is reacting" simply says that the source of the action is in the total play environment, not just within your character.

It is this interrelatedness of all character activities, both verbal and nonverbal, which moves the entire play. Each of your character's actions causes a *reaction* either in another character, or within your own character, or both. Each *reaction* serves in turn as a new *action*, causing yet another reaction, and so on. In this way, the interaction of the characters in their situation moves forward the plot of the play.

Your character's participation in the plot of his play can be described as a *hierarchy* of actions, ranging from individual *moments*, which work together to form logical units of action called *beats*, the beats working together to form *scenes*, the scenes working together to form the over-all or *main* action of the role. You must analyze each of these levels as you prepare your performance. Compare the hierarchy of dramatic activities to the structure of a piece of literature: Phrases make up sentences, just as *momentary activities* make up logical units of action called *beats*; sentences make up paragraphs, just as beats string together to make a *scene*; paragraphs work together to develop a story's main theme, just as your scenes work together to express the *main action* of your role.

The *main action* of a role is its over-all dramatic purpose in *actable* terms. This main action was called the *super-objective* by Stanislavski:

> We use the word super-objective to characterize the essential idea, the core, which provided the impetus for the writing of a play. . . . In a play the whole stream of individual minor objectives, all the imaginative thoughts, feelings, and actions of an actor should converge to carry out this super-objective. . . . Also this impetus toward the super-objective must be continuous throughout the whole play.[30]

Sometimes this is also called the "through-line" or the "spine" of a character. We use the term *main action*, because it emphasizes a dynamic and outgoing quality of stage activity.

It is not always easy to describe a role's main action, since it may be very complex and may even undergo several changes in the course of the play. The important thing, however, is to express it in *active* terms, and to understand how it enables the character to realize his dramatic purpose as a contributor to the plot and meaning of the play. Your description of your role's main action should not only guide you about *what* to do, but also provide an idea about *how* it must be done in order to contribute as much as possible.

The main action often will be understood only after all the component actions of which it is made have been explored and experienced, and even

---

[30] Stanislavski, *An Actor's Handbook*, pp. 137–38.

then it may remain inexpressable. Nevertheless, it is that over-all understanding of where the character is heading that alone can provide coherence and unity to your performance.

The action of each *scene* may be easier to grasp and to express. Usually a character will have one general action in a scene, which will be worked out through the *beats* that form logical units within the scene action, and the *momentary* actions of which the beats are made. The actor's immediate concern when performing is to fulfill each moment as it happens, but this is only after each moment has been understood as contributing to a beat, each beat to a scene, and each scene to the main action.

You can understand the interrelatedness of all your moments only when you understand the *dramatic purpose* they serve, as well as the quality of your *character's action*, which they express. The playwright has made your job easier, of course, by providing a multitude of actions implicit in the verbal structure of the play, and the kind of close textual analysis you have already learned will go far toward helping you to understand your character's actions on every level.

SHAPING THE ACTION

The main action, and indeed, each of the levels of character action, has a shape of its own, which may be compared to the shape of a piece of music. It begins at a certain point and we sense its direction; it progresses and develops in complexity and richness, and usually increases in tension until it reaches a crisis at which the tension must be resolved (whether it is or not; in many contemporary plays it is not). Sensing the almost musical shaping of action on every level is an important quality in good acting, and it provides you with the indispensible ability of *preparing* an action as well as simply performing it. In most plays, in fact, the effectiveness of an action on any of the levels we have just described depends more upon the clarity of the process that culminates in the action than upon the performance of the action itself.

In a production of Brecht's *Mother Courage*, for example, an actress playing the role of Kattrin, the mute daughter, asked me for help in analyzing the action of her last scene. In it, Kattrin climbs atop a hut and beats a drum, so as to warn the nearby town of an impending attack. The soldiers coax and threaten her in every way they can, trying to make her stop her drumming. Finally, she is shot. Clearly, this scene and the action of choosing to warn the town is the climax of her entire performance. Yet no scene is easier to do *if* the preparation is correct. If the audience has been shown all the things that make this action understandable and indeed inevitable, there is almost no way the scene can be done badly. The impact of a moment, of a scene, of an entire role, is the payoff made by careful investment in preparation. You may reap only what you have previously sown.

Therefore, understanding the process that precedes every action is essential to an effective performance. This process involves understanding *how* each moment contributes to its beat, *how* each beat contributes to its scene, and each scene to the main action of the role, and the role to the entire play.

In this case, the actress should examine each moment of her role, each of her previous actions and reactions, to see how it will contribute to this final action, since this final action embodies the ultimate development and fullest possible statement of Kattrin's being. It is also, of course, the final fulfillment of her dramatic purpose, since hers is the only truly *selfless* act in the entire play. By her sacrifice, by the fact that the world of the play makes it mandatory that a humane action is also suicidal, we are able to see the other characters and their world in sharper perspective.

Kattrin's dramatic purpose is to provide one glimmer of selflessness against which the avarice and callousness of the other characters, against which a world in which love itself has been outlawed by economic necessity, may be judged. Her main action is *to observe* the various ways in which people are forced to abandon their humanity in order to "get along," and finally *to protest* what she has seen when she can no longer countenance such a world. Each of her scenes, beats, and moments must be understood as contributing to this main action; further, the *way* in which each action is performed must be designed to fulfill the dramatic purpose for which each action was devised.

So far, we have been discussing the "surface" of dramatic action, and it is necessary to examine also the processes of thought and feeling underlying such action. It is necessary, too, to remember that in *some* plays the quality of the action itself is less external than the sort we have been discussing here; but whether the action is more or less "interior," whether it is more or less supported by psychological processes, it is still the *action* itself, and not the character who serves the action, that is the essence of drama. Remembering this, we will proceed to examine the "interior" of character in the next lesson as a further extension and support of dramatic action; but first perform this exercise in the analysis and realization of action.

Group Exercise 8: Structure and Action
Polarization

With a partner, choose a short scene from a play which you have both studied carefully in its entirety. Be sure the scene you choose expresses one complete unit of scene action. Each of you should memorize it thoroughly. Then perform the following exercise:

Part I: Close Text Analysis

1. Working together, analyze the diction of the scene according to the material in Lesson 8. If it is from an old play, or a highly colloquial one, write a paraphrase. Be sure that each of you understands the diction of *all* the speeches, not merely your own.
2. In the same way, analyze the rhythms of the scene jointly. Pay special attention to the rhythm established by the alternation of the dialogue and the tempo changes implied by the emotional shaping of the scene.
3. Analyze jointly the vocal melody of the scene. In all these analyses, discuss the implications of what you discover for the shape of the scene, the purpose, and the scene action of each of the characters.
4. Continue your analysis and discussion of the imagery and the figurative language. Be sure you understand what reactions are demanded of your individual characters to the meaning, rhythm and tone, imagery, and figurative language of the other character.
5. What is the *shape* of the energies of the scene? If you were to liken it to a piece of music, what kind would it be?

Part II: Scene Analysis

Study and discuss the entire play and answer the following questions about it and about your scene:

1. What is the principal source of the play's *organization*? How is the plot organized? Which are the central characters? How does your scene reflect this?
2. What is the underlying *theme* or themes of the play, and how does your scene contribute to it?
3. What is the basic *conflict* of the play? What is the basic conflict of your scene, and how does it advance the movement of the whole play?
4. Considering each of your characters in the entire play, what are their *main actions* and *main dramatic purposes*?
5. Within this scene, what is the *scene action* and *dramatic purpose* of each of your characters?
6. What are the *beats* that make up the scene? How is each related to dramatic purpose?
7. What are the *momentary actions* that make up each beat? How is each related to dramatic purpose?

Part III: Action Polarization

1. Scene Rhythm

A. Choose an *over-all pattern of movement*, a sort of rough "blocking" expressed as principles of movement, that expresses the *scene action* (for example, one character is trying to pry something out of the other, so one will remain closed up or continually in retreat, while the other pursues and attempts various movement-strategies to penetrate the defenses of the other. Here, the actions of *prying* and *penetrating* versus *retreating* and *closing up* would be literally acted out.).

B. Choose *individual movement patterns* that express qualities or needs of each character (for example, the aggressive character might be *open* and *free* in his movements, while the other is *heavy* and *inhibited* in his).

C. Using your individual pattern *within* the over-all pattern, attempt to recreate the shape of the scene, using *only* full organic movement, vocal noise (not words), and uninhibited physical contact. Each of you pursue your character actions in reaction to the other. Be especially careful to realize the shape of each beat and the patterning of the beats to form the scene. Use the rhythms, sounds, and dominant sensations, which you analyzed in Part I of this exercise, as the *basis* for your movement and noise, but don't try to be too specific. Concentrate instead on the *action* of the scene.

CAUTION: The aim of this exercise is, like the other polarizations, to create a total organic experience of the action of the scene. Seek out every opportunity for exaggerated movement and noise and react fully and physically to each other. Do not be tied to "realistic" movement or even to the type of movement that might really be used in the performance of the scene. Your aim here is EXPERIENCE, *not* PERFORMANCE.

2. VERBALIZING THE SCENE

When you both feel that you have realized the shaping of the scene and have honestly communicated *real* cause/effect energies to each other through your actions and reactions, begin to allow the energies of your noise and movement to shape themselves into the words of the scene. Don't force the words to come, just push them a little. If your organic involvement is complete and your analysis has been correct, the words should begin coming as a natural extension and completion of your action.

Keep a firm sense of the *process of verbalization* as an active decision-making one, which is an integral part of the action and thought of the character. Be sure to respond fully to the growing verbalization of your partner as well.

Characterization

Now that we have explored the shaping of a character's action and the dramatic purposes it serves, let us explore the components of characterization itself and those thoughts and feelings of a character that lie below the surface of an action and below the surface of the text itself.

Characterization is a means to an end, never an end in itself. Your creation of the character is really the *measure* of how successfully you have performed the tasks we have been studying so far, how successfully you perform certain actions in certain specific ways. In other words, the creation of character is not the job you *set out* to do, it is rather what you *end up* with when you have done all your various tasks well.

CHARACTERIZATION

To help him serve his dramatic purpose and to perform his actions believably, a character is constructed in a specific way. He is provided with certain traits relating to his actions and purposes, and to help distinguish him from, and to cause him to effectively interact with, the other characters in the play.

We can classify these characterizational traits on four levels, as suggested here by Oscar Brockett:

> Character is the material from which plots are created, for incidents are developed mainly through the speech and behavior of dramatic personages. Characterization is the playwright's means of differentiating one dramatic personage from another. Since a dramatist may endow his creatures with few or many traits, complexity of characterization varies markedly. In analyzing roles, it is helpful to look at four levels of characterization. (This approach is adapted from a scheme suggested by Hubert Heffner in *Modern Theatre Practice* and elsewhere.)
>
> The first level of characterization is *physical* and is concerned only with such basic facts as sex, age, size, and color. Sometimes a dramatist does not supply all of this information, but it is present whenever the play is produced, since actors necessarily give concrete form to the characters. The physical is the simplest level of characterization, however, since it

reveals external traits only, many of which may not affect the dramatic action at all.

The second level is *social*. It includes a character's economic status, profession or trade, religion, family relationships—all those factors which place him in his environment.

The third level is *psychological*. It reveals a character's habitual responses, attitudes, desires, motivations, likes and dislikes—the inner workings of the mind, both emotional and intellectual, which precede action. Since habits of feeling, thought, and behavior define characters more fully than do physical and social traits, and since drama most often arises from conflicting desires, the psychological is the most essential level of characterization.

The fourth level is *moral*. Although implied in all plays, it is not always emphasized. It is most apt to be used in serious plays, especially tragedies. Although almost all human action suggests some ethical standard, in many plays the moral implications are ignored and decisions are made on grounds of expediency. This is typical of comedy, since moral deliberations tend to make any action serious. More nearly than any other kind, moral decisions differentiate characters, since the choices they make when faced with moral crises show whether they are selfish, hypocritical, or persons of integrity. A moral decision usually causes a character to examine his own motives and values, in the process of which his true nature is revealed both to himself and to the audience.[31]

PHYSICAL TRAITS

Let us examine these four levels of characterization more fully. The first level is *physical*, and while it may be the simplest level in relation to dramatic action, it is certainly of primary importance to an actor. The physical or external traits of body and voice that you present to your audience are the *only* means by which you can communicate any of the other levels of characterization. There is no "mental telepathy" in the theatre; if the audience can't *see* it or *hear* it, they can't understand it or feel it.

This is *not* to say that there is one right or wrong way for a character to look and sound. Except for a few essential traits demanded by the play, there is considerable latitude for an actor to use his own voice and body to best advantage in a role. For example, a skinny Falstaff is inconceivable, but are we really sure that Hamlet has to be thin? Willy Loman is described by Arthur Miller as being a slight man, yet the powerfully built Lee J. Cobb created a masterpiece in his portrayal of the salesman.

The Elizabethans believed that a person's physical characteristics expressed his personality; they would expect a man with a "bovine" face to be slow of

---

[31] Brockett, *The Theatre: An Introduction*, p. 34.

wit. Falstaff's fatness is an important expression of the "fatness" of his spirit; generous and good-humored, but also lazy, sloppy, and irresponsible. In many ways, we still respond strongly to physical traits in this way; psychologists have actually determined that a squat or large-abdomened man (an "endomorph") is indeed often easy-going, jolly, and a good "family man," while the "athletic" build (the "mesomorph") and the thin, nervous type (the "ectomorph") often exhibit qualities popularly associated with their types. So within very wide limits, a basic appropriateness of body to a role is advantageous, but this should never be construed as an argument for "type-casting."

The physical qualities of character specified by most plays are general and malleable enough to make "type-casting" artistically unnecessary. Stanley Kowalski ought to have a strongly masculine physique and "animalistic" quality, and many actors who simply could not achieve these qualities would be disqualified for this role. Nevertheless, these qualities could be manifested in many ways by many actors, most of whom would have only ordinary physiques. The important point here is that while physical traits are a way of expressing the nature of the character, they do not have specific meanings of their own. The audience will usually accept *your* way of manifesting an important physical trait. Lee J. Cobb's body is solid and powerful, yet through his posture, rhythms, and muscle tone, he created a vivid impression of Willy Loman's exhaustion and frailty. Within the boundaries of common sense, what you've *got* is not as important as how you *use* it.

Your participation in the basic physical traits of the character is a powerful "trigger," which can generate a deeper sense of involvement in the thought and emotion of the character. Many actors use a walk, a posture, or a style of gesture as the starting point for their creation. No amount of intellectual or psychological analysis will replace the actual *experiencing* of the character which can occur when you begin to adopt his physical traits, assuming that these traits are accurate expressions of the other levels of characterizations, and also relate to the potential of your own body and voice.

Don't underestimate the contribution that can be made by make-up and costuming. Age and physique can be changed radically. But padding and crepe hair can only *support* a physical characterization, never *substitute* for one. Any costume and make-up depends upon the actor's skill in wearing it, while no good actor has ever *depended* upon costume and make-up. Nevertheless, such aids are respectable and important elements of your theatrical heritage, and it would be stupid to avoid using whatever can help to create a more vivid character.

It is important to take into account costume, make-up, and properties when preparing a role and to rehearse with substitutes and the actual things thoroughly. The most wonderfully complete characterizations can be ruined by lack of familiarity with a prop or costume, or by failure to adjust to or capitalize on make-up. These things involve great technical skill, however, and require special study in your future training. Too much too soon is deadly, as described in this wonderful section on how to steal-a-scene-even-with-a-tiny-part, from Michael Green's spoof on acting textbooks, *Downwind of Upstage*:

> Askew's cousin Watkins had merely to walk across the stage as a bystander in a street scene. When he went on, there was such a gasp from the audience that I thought he must have made a rude sign at the balcony. . . . When I peered from the wings I saw why he had caused such a sensation. He had put real character into the part. To start with he had strapped one leg up and was walking with a crutch. He wore dark glasses and carried a placard—"Blind." He had put on a false nose so revolting that one could not describe it. Boils were plastered all over his face and there was a great bruise on his forehead which looked like a third eye. No one could miss him.
>
> Directors do not take kindly to this sort of thing, so it cannot be too strongly emphasized that no hint must be given before the first night. . . . The director, by the way, kicked up an awful fuss and took away his crutches, so next night Watkins was towed in on a little trolley like Porgy in the Gershwin musical. For some reason we never saw the director again after that, but he still writes to us from Canada . . . .
>
> As a comparatively young actor I had a part in *King John* as Second Citizen of Angiers. I was carefully sorting out various sticks of make-up when I noticed that the First Citizen had mixed together a fetid sort of mud pie from every stick in his box, and was plastering it all over his face.
>
> "I believe in experiment," he said thickly through the cake which covered his features. "After all, I reckon you've got to be pretty old to become First Citizen of an important place like Angiers."
>
> The effect of this apparition rising over the battlements of the beleaguered city would have struck fear into the stoutest heart. King John visibly quailed, while the Duke of Austria burst into laughter (although this was partly due to his having drunk three bottles of beer before he went on). It was a lesson I never forgot. . . . There is no compromise. One is young or senile, fit or crippled. The younger an actor is, the older and more decrepit he tries to be. I have seen school shows with entire armies of limping men.[32]

At this stage of your development, you must be content with the basic qualities of physical characterization, which: 1) *are described in the stage direction,* 2) *described by other characters,* 3) *can be deduced from the action of the play, or from the close text analysis you have learned,* which will supply many suggestions about the posture, rhythms, and vocal qualities of the character.

---

[32] Michael Green, *Downwind of Upstage: The Art of Coarse Acting* (New York: Hawthorn Books, Inc., 1966), pp. 44–45.

From each of these sources, you look for physical qualities which: 1) *relate to the action the character must perform*, 2) *express the personality of the character*, or 3) *relate to the style of the play*. This last point is a very advanced one, but for now you can consider it on a basic level; a character in a Restoration comedy, for example, had better not slouch around like someone in *The Iceman Cometh*, and *vice versa*.

In relation to each of these points, you further ask yourself the crucial questions, *how will I use my body and voice to manifest the traits required of the character? What do I experience by participating in the physical traits of the character?*

SOCIAL TRAITS

This second level of characterization relates the character to his environment and the people in it. Character can be understood fully only when we understand the situation in which it operates. Even a single emotion cannot be properly interpreted without an understanding of context. This fact has been recognized by psychologists:

> The celebrated James-Lange theory of emotion as a reaction to bodily movement—for instance running away gives rise to fear or weeping gives rise to sorrow—is half right. What needs to be added is that the bodily actions or condition are also a relevant *orientation to*, and a potential *manipulation of*, the environment; for example, it is not just running, but running *away*, running away from *something*, running away from something *dangerous*, that contributes to the situation of fear.[33]

We must never, even on a basic emotional level, approach our characters in a vacuum. Only by fully realizing the situation and relationships, the objectives, the inhibitions, and the characteristic responses of our character can we fully understand the emotions to be expressed in our performance. The playwright has carefully chosen and constructed the situation in which the characters operate, and it is our job to discover the essential aspects of that situation that influence character.

Many of Tennessee Williams' plays, for example, must take place in the hot, humid climate of the south. Think what an air-conditioner would do to Blanche Dubois! Shakespeare chose to set a play of great passion, *Othello*, in a similar climate. But beyond simple physical influences of climate, the *social* environment established by the playwright is of great importance. The society in which Stanley Kowalski moves, for example, is an active part of Stanley's character. Think over the plays you have read, and you will see how in each case the influences of the immediate locale have been carefully chosen and are indispensible ingredients in the realization of character.

---

[33] Perls, Hefferline, and Goodman, *Gestalt Therapy*, p. 98.

Even more important than the effect of the environment is the character's relationship to each of the other characters in the play. The relationships are a direct expression of the conflict or dramatic interaction between the participants, and also a profound influence upon and expression of each of their individual characters. When we examine one of these relationships, we see an extraordinary wealth of information that is in many ways more important to the actor than statements about each of the characters alone. As in life, dramatic characters achieve their fullest sense of identity only through their interaction with others. Your concept of a character and the determination of his dramatic function and main action must be based on an understanding of his purposeful interaction with other characters, as expressed by his relationships.

In *Death of a Salesman*, Willy has a relationship with each person in the play; father, husband, lover, neighbor, employee, salesman. We see Willy operating in each of these contexts, and each relationship reveals another aspect of Willy's character. Each of these relationships also helps us to penetrate through the surface of his behavior to the underlying consistency of Willy's character.

As we define our character's various actions and desires at any moment, we must define his relationships and what they are expressing as well. Our reactions, which in turn become new actions, will grow almost entirely within the context and pressure provided by these relationships.

As is often said to actors, "the roots of what you do is in the other people," and realizing the character's relationship to each of the other characters provides the guidelines for your interaction with your co-workers as well as tremendous insight into the character itself. Examine your role and ask yourself: 1) *What is my character's relationship to his environment?* 2) *What is his relationship to every other character?* 3) *How does each of these relationships affect his dramatic purpose?* 4) *How does each of these relationships affect his needs, desires, and intentions?* 5) *How does each affect his actions?*

PSYCHOLOGICAL AND MORAL TRAITS

We will approach the third and fourth levels of characterization as one. We must here understand the *process of thought*, which is the precedent of action. The nature of this process is different, and serves different functions, in various plays. In plays where the external action of the plot itself is the dominant element of the play (as in allegories, farces, and some Classical tragedies, for example), the psychological aspect of characterization is of small importance. In fact, when the actor insists on psychologically motivating every action, even when such motivation is irrelevant to the nature of the play, the quality of the play's structure may greatly suffer. On the other hand, some plays feature *interior* action (like those of Chekhov and O'Neill for example) and here the psychology of the characters is the vehicle for the plot itself.

The main point is to remember that the psychology of character is meant always to serve the demands of *action*, and that the relative importance and nature of psychological characterization is dependent on the play's dramatic objectives and structure. Having stated this, let us proceed to examine the internal operations of a character's thought, remembering that these principles are applied very differently in different plays.

Each action grows out of, relates to, and in turn affects the character's *thought* and feeling. It is not so much that a character's thought *motivates* his actions (in *some* plays they do), but rather that a character's thought is part and parcel of his action. If we fail to provide the audience with an understanding of the thought that is part of an action, we have not only failed to prepare for the action adequately, we have also failed to present the action in its completeness.

In most plays, a character's thought (and we include in this one term his feelings as well; we mean, really, his *consciousness*) is a dynamic process of decision, which culminates in action. This process involves the character's needs, desires, and intentions, his ethical nature, and his responsiveness to his environment and the way in which it frustrates or excites his needs. The process by which a character attempts to satisfy his needs and desires and is frustrated by his situation is much like the process by which personality is formed in real life. By understanding a character's way of responding to frustration or difficulty, we will discover an active and expressive sense of his personality.

The obstacles that frustrate a character's objectives serve an important dramatic purpose. If a character's objectives were immediately realized, plays would be very short indeed; we depend on the shaping of dramatic *tensions* to sustain interest and movement in a play, and it is the frustration of objectives that produces tension.

As our desire to achieve a goal is frustrated, tension results, and that tension is eventually resolved in action, which in its turn is either successful or the source of new tensions. A character's objectives and his selection of the means to overcome the obstacles to his goals are the dynamic process that leads him to action and an active expression of his personality.

At the inception of an action, there is a *felt need*, some basic desire or objective. The character then surveys the alternatives available to him for satisfying that need, alternatives presented him by his situation. When he selects one of the alternatives, his decision will vividly express his character.

Also, the words spoken in the dialogue are themselves activities, which are the result of decisions made during the process of verbalization. A character's *diction*, his choice of words to express himself, is itself a result of the whole process of thought underlying each dramatic activity.

Once a decision has been made, action will usually follow. This resultant action is, in dramatic terms, the most important part of this process, but only because in a good play and performance, the audience is aware of the entire *process* that has culminated in the action.

We should also remember that everything we say about the process of thought underlying an action also applies to a character's *reactions*. In a reaction, the starting point of the process of thought is an external event rather than an internal need or desire. But the external event immediately relates to the character's needs, and the way in which he reacts to this event is a result of the same process of thought we have been describing.

In Arthur Miller's *Death of a Salesman*, for example, Willy, whose felt need is to be "successful," is presented by his situation with several alternatives. He could, like his brother Ben, strike off on some bold venture; or he could, like his neighbor Charley, accept his life as it is and see that in many important ways he *is* a success. But Willy is driven by the "American Dream," in which success is not internal satisfaction, but the esteem of others and the tangible worth of material possessions. Lacking the courage and independence to follow his brother's example, and lacking also the sense of self-identity necessary to accept his own lot, he finally opts for a third alternative, the suicide, which will give his insurance to his family. It is the making of this choice, and seeing how frustrations from society and from within Willy himself have driven him to this choice, which moves the entire mechanism of the play.

In the terms we have been using, Willy's *main dramatic purpose* relates to the *theme* of his play; how American society in general, and the free enterprise system in particular, can destroy a man by filling him with false values. The *main action* that translates this dramatic purpose into active terms is Willy's constant *search for "success,"* which for him means esteem and possessions. Each scene, each beat, each moment of the role, and Willy's thought at any moment, can be understood as contributing to this basic purpose, and reflecting this main action.

When the process of a character's decision-making involves moral values, as it does in Willy's case, then we can speak of his ethical or moral characterization. When this aspect of character is important, it will always relate directly to the thematic content of the play; the moral choice confronting Willy, for example, is an embodiment of Arthur Miller's thesis regarding American society. When such moral value is attached to your character, you must shape your performance to meet its demands, though the *process* of thought involved will be the same as that we have already described. In other words, the psychological and moral levels of characterization are not different in *kind*, but only in the *values* involved.

COMPLEXITY OF
CHARACTERIZATION

We have examined each of four levels of characterization. Each works in relation to each of the others, and the way in which they are put together reflects the purpose and nature of the play. Oscar Brockett indicates this:

> A playwright may emphasize one or more of these levels. Some writers pay little attention to the physical appearance of their characters, concentrating instead upon psychological and moral traits; other dramatists may describe appearance and social status in detail. In assessing the completeness of a characterization, however, it is not enough merely to make a list of traits and levels of characterization. It is also necessary to ask *how the character functions in the play*. For example, the audience needs to know little about the maid who only appears to announce dinner; any detailed characterization would be superflous and distracting. On the other hand, the principal characters need to be drawn in greater depth. The appropriateness and completeness of each characterization, therefore, may be judged only after analyzing its function in each scene and in the play as a whole.[34]

Too often we train actors as if each of them were going to play nothing but major roles, and so they attempt to turn the maid announcing dinner into Phaedra. This is not to say that the maid should not be fully characterized; she should be as fully characterized as *she needs to be*. To realize the limits of a characterization and fill them completely, without allowing extraneous and irrelevant details to obscure the clear outlines of dramatic purpose and character action, is what we mean by *economy*.

Think of a great athlete whose performances you have admired. His "style," his grace and power, come from the complete *efficiency* with which every bit of his energy is focused upon the job at hand. He exhibits no movement or bit of concentration that does not directly contribute to his purpose. This is his economy.

If *your* purpose is to be a maid announcing dinner, then any energy directed toward creating qualities beyond those necessary for the fulfillment of this task are wasteful and distracting. An overly detailed performance is as disruptive as an incomplete one. This is the actor's sense of economy, and it is the hallmark of his skill and concentration.

---

[34] Brockett, *The Theatre: An Introduction*, p. 35.

THE DYNAMIC NATURE OF
CHARACTER

Just as your personality in real life is continually changing, many dramatic characters are shown undergoing a similar process. Not all characters change, of course; despite the tremendously moving things that happen to them and the shattering discoveries they make about themselves. Oedipus, Othello, Jerry in *The Zoo Story*, and many other important characters from every type of drama undergo no essential change of character within their plays. Minor characters are rarely characterized deeply enough to undergo significant changes, and since such change usually implies some serious self-discovery, comic characters rarely change in any essential way.

When a significant change in the nature of a dramatic character *is* demanded, however, it is often a direct expression of a theme of the play, and the dramatic purpose of many characters is to undergo just such a change. In these cases, the main action should be defined in terms of the change, and all minor activities defined in terms of their contribution to the change.

Lear, for example, undergoes a radical change, which is expressed in three phases: his self-centeredness at the outset of the play, the suffering and madness he brings upon himself in the middle of the play, and the humility and love of humanity he has learned by the end. It is hard to imagine the Lear of the first scene praying for justice for the poor, or calling himself a "fond, foolish old man."

Yet it is this change in Lear that expresses the main theme of the play and is Lear's dramatic function. His main action changes, then, as he changes. At first, his main activity is to retire as king and still be assured of grace, comfort, and respect. All his actions in the first two acts can be related to this activity, which is frustrated by his daughters. When this desire has been completely frustrated, the second unit of action begins, as Lear himself prophesies, "O, fool, I shall go mad."

Lear's second main action is to seek vengeance upon his daughters, and the storm is at once a heavenly extension of his wrath and a punishment for his earlier pride and insensitivity. Throughout his growing madness, he seeks vengeance, this main action sustaining him until his meeting with Gloucester near the end of the fourth act, when he imagines sneaking up on his daughters, "Then, kill, kill, kill, kill, kill, kill!"

His third and last main action is expressed in his love for Cordelia, a poetic balancing, since it was his banishing of Cordelia that instigated the tragedy in Scene 1. The man who was self-centered at the outset of the play has, through suffering, become completely *other*-centered in his love for his daughter at the end, and the shifting of his main actions reflects the change.

Lear's change embodies the change in his world, away from the injustice of feudal society toward a more humanistic, democratic morality.

Group Exercise 9: Thought Polarization

Use the same scene you and your partner chose for the previous exercise. Considering the entire play, as well as the demands of your particular scene, consider each level of the characterization of your roles.

I. PHYSICAL:

What physical characteristics are important to your role? Consider stage directions, descriptions by other characters, and information you can deduce from the purposes and actions of your character.

II. SOCIAL:

A. What factors of environment are important to your characters?
B. What relationship do your characters have in the play? In this scene? In each beat of this scene?
C. How do these relationships help express your characters' dramatic purposes?
D. How do they influence your actions?

III. PSYCHOLOGICAL AND MORAL:

A. Considering the entire play—
   1. Does your play feature mainly external or internal action? How important is psychological characterization to it?
   2. What are the needs, desires or intentions of each of your characters? How does their relationship affect or express these needs?
   3. What alternatives are available to your characters for the satisfaction of their needs?
   4. On what basis do the characters choose between these alternatives? Are moral choices involved? What do their choices express?
   5. How does this process of thought lead to the actions of the characters? How does it help express their dramatic purpose?
   6. How detailed and complex must each of your characterizations be in order to be appropriate to the meaning, organization, and style of the play?
B. Considering your scene in particular—
   1. How does the relationship between your characters affect the scene action?
   2. How does the psychological process of each character affect the scene action?
      a. Relate your character's immediate need, intention, or desire to the scene action.
      b. What decisions does he make within the scene, if any?

    c. How do his reactions to the situation or to the
       other character express his thought and affect the action?
3. Consider each beat of the scene and each moment of each beat. How does this organization of the scene action help express the process of thought of each character?

IV. THOUGHT POLARIZATION:

Act out the scene slowly, trying to *exteriorize* the process of thought of each character. Let the audience see your character's needs or intentions, the alternatives available to him, and the decisions he makes prior to each of his actions or reactions. In other words, physicalize *as a muscular experience* the dynamic process of thought of your character. Again, your movements will not be "realistic" or even appropriate to a performance of the scene. Instead, move so as to create *for yourself and your partner* an active expression of your character's thought. See how fully you can respond to, and participate in, your partner's thought as well; experience how the movement of the scene is produced by the interaction of the thought processes of the characters.

Putting Yourself into the Character

Is the character that you play a sort of mask, having a separate identity of its own, which you stand behind and bring to life by making it move and speak? Or does the character become your own face, involving your own being?

Stanislavski told his actors, "always be yourself on stage." On the other hand, some actors concentrate on the external appearance of their characters, as if the character were "someone else." Several surveys of British and American actors have shown that they are fairly evenly divided between those whose approach is mainly subjective, working from "internals," and those who concentrate more upon "externals."

Most actors work with an awareness of both. The creation of a vital stage performance must involve the actor's own feelings in some way, but all the "internal truth" in the world will be useless, if the externals presented to the audience are inaccurate or technically deficient. On the other hand, the best technique can only serve, and never substitute for, an actor's personal creative energy.

A character existing only on the printed page of your script is lifeless. At first he is only an outline, an empty receptacle waiting to be filled. You must contribute your responses, give something of your own vitality, in order to bring him to life. Many external properties of the receptacle have been determined by the playwright. You create the energy that will, for you, best fill the receptacle, best make it glow with inner life, though you must make your contribution flow naturally into the outlines provided by the playwright.

The actor must *analyze, respond to,* and *rejuvenate* what the playwright provides. This process is a dialogue between externals and internals, each affecting the other, with the text as the initiator and eventual criterion of judgment of this process.

Though your own feelings must be engaged in the creation of the character, they must be selected and modified in order to meet the demands of the script. *You do not absorb the character into yourself but, rather, put yourself into the character.*

USE OF YOUR OWN EXPERIENCE

Your own feelings and experiences are the principal materials you manipulate in fashioning a creation appropriate to the demands of a given play, but it would be irresponsible to force a character to conform to your personality. The actor's art is a very creative one, but it is not a particularly *self*-expressive one. Perhaps we should say that *the actor realizes himself by living the life of his characters.*

Since most human experience has some commonality, a good deal of your own experience will be useful in the creation of any character. But the way in which that experience is used, the configuration it assumes, must be determined by the demands of the play, not by the nature of your own being.

Remember also that most plays deal with situations that are in part extraordinary, or beyond your specific life experience. When you do old plays, for example, you are forced to relive the spirit of an age that has long since ceased to be, to behave in a way that is alien to the "natural" behavior of your own time. Even contemporary plays demand a great deal that you cannot provide from your own real experience, and it will be a rare occurrence when your own habitual manner of expression will satisfactorily coincide with the form required by a particular play.

A sense of estrangement and the thought of suicide has at some time crossed the minds of most of us, but we have not behaved precisely like Jerry, nor done what Jerry does in *The Zoo Story*. Nevertheless, your own emotional *energies*, if not the habitual form in which you express them, provide the basis of all stage creation, remembering that however much you may utilize your own experience and feelings in creating a part, you will also gain *new* experience and feelings in the process.

This is one of the most exciting aspects of acting: The actor is continually expanding himself, continually having experiences that are inaccessible to the average person. By feeling what it is to live in past ages, in other places, and inside of people quite different from ourselves, actors find their own lives continually challenged and expanded. The actor who looks *only* within himself for the materials of creation is robbing himself of vast riches of experience embodied within the great plays of the theatre; the actor who, on the other hand, refuses to involve himself in his creation, will remain unaffected by the experiences he pretends to be having.

THE ACTOR AND HIS CHARACTER : EMPATHY

The way in which an actor projects himself *into* his character is not unlike the way in which we put ourselves "in the shoes" of other people in real life. Psychologists call this process *empathy*. The word "empathy" has been knocking around the theatre for a good many years. No one is quite sure what it means, and it is so misused that some critics have suggested abandoning it altogether. If we look into the development of this concept, however, we can find much that seems useful as a way of describing the actor-character relationship.

The word "empathy" was coined in 1906 to translate the German word, *einfühlung*. *Einfühlung* literally means "in-feeling," and it originally described how we project muscular sensations into inanimate objects. When we look at a steeple "thrusting" up toward the sky, sense the "twisting" feeling of a spiral, or the "rolling" feeling of low hills, we are projecting these muscular feelings *into* the objects. Later on, psychologists began to use this term as a way of describing how a person can imaginatively project himself into the place of another person. When you are empathizing, you are feeling yourself "in" the place of another person, though the feelings you are experiencing are still your own, not his.

> You can share an experience with someone in the sense that you and he may experience similarly some situation which you and he have in common but what he experiences is *his* and what you experience is *yours*. When you say to a friend in trouble, "I feel for you," you do not mean that literally, since he is doing his own feeling and no one else can do it for him, but simply that you, by imagining yourself in his place, construct a vivid picture of what the situation would be like—and then react to that.[35]

Recently, however, empathy has come to be regarded as a much more complex process, which can lead to a profound participation in another's existence. In order to explain this more complex view of empathy, we must first clarify several other terms: *sympathy*, *imitation*, and *identification*. Commonly misused in the theatre, often as synonyms, these terms have fairly precise definitions in psychology.

SYMPATHY. Sympathy and empathy are two different concepts. It is true that we usually empathize with someone with whom we sympathize, but it is not necessary to sympathize in order to empathize. Sympathy implies a strong sense of *agreement* with another person, while empathy does not necessarily involve agreement or even liking. When the villain is kicked in the pants, we empathetically stiffen and cringe, though we way be delighted at the same time. It is possible, of course, that strong empathy can *lead* to sympathy by helping us to realize vividly the other fellow's point of view.

This is not always the function of empathy in the theatre, however. In *King Lear*, Edmund the bastard makes us understand his point of view very well, and he is such a vivid personality that our empathy with him will probably be quite strong. It would be unfortunate for a proper understanding of the play, however, if we began to sympathize with him unduly.

---

[35] Perls, Hefferline, and Goodman, *Gestalt Therapy*, p. 33.

IMITATION AND IDENTIFICATION. The idea of "imitation" is defined by psychologists as a simple physical mimicry of one person for another. When we are in the company of someone we greatly admire, for example, we may assume his mannerisms temporarily, his way of speaking, or even his way of thinking. We are imitating him, but only on a relatively superficial level. Our imitation has not profoundly changed our own identity. If, however, our identity *is* profoundly influenced by someone else, then we "identify" with that person. In identification, there is a deep and permanent alteration of our own personality under the influence of another ego. We often say that an audience "identifies" with a character, but as you can see, a case of true identification in the theatre would be a rare and perhaps wonderful event, though a profound identification with someone like Jerry in *The Zoo Story* might have unpleasant results.

Imitating someone superficially may help us to feel closer to him and, if conditions are right, may help us to develop identification. As Freud put it, "Imitation, through empathy, can lead to identification." Empathy, therefore, is the active *process* by which we progress from a simple, imitative relationship to a more profound one.

Sometimes such identification can take on the qualities of a very meaningful relationship when it does not limit the communication only to ways in which the participants are similar. Such identification involves *respect* for each other's *separate* identities, *at the same time* that you relate strongly to one another. In this way, each person's identity is enhanced. Imitation concentrates solely upon *similarities*, while identification takes into account *both* similarities *and* dissimilarities, giving each participant a heightened and more truthful awareness of his partner's being.

The empathic process is the *balancing*, then, of imitation and respect, of our awareness of our similarities and our separateness, leading to identification. This description of empathy is useful for comparing the relationship of actor and character in various forms of theatre. The naturalistic theatre tends to emphasize imitation, encouraging the actor to concentrate on the similarities between himself and the character, to get as "close" to the character as possible. In classical and much contemporary theatre, however, a sense of the character's separate existence as a mythic *stage creation* is emphasized by a presentational style. All forms of theatre, of course, involve a balancing of both imitation and respect, in whatever proportions are appropriate to the form of the play.

The good actor strives to identify with his character in the best sense of the word. If he concentrates *only* on the ways in which he is similar to his character, then he is merely imitating. While it *is* necessary for you to search out all the ways in which you are similar to your character, to bring to bear all experiences that help you to understand and express the character, it would be foolish and unrealistic to ignore the many ways in which you and your character are quite different, especially in the form of your expression and that demanded by the character. These differences must be realized, accepted, and utilized.

You must isolate the aspects of your own experience and behavior that are not appropriate to the creation of the character, and extend or modify them in the act of creation until they *are* appropriate. It is all too easy to imitate a character so strongly that you project into him qualities of your own personality and experience, which turn out to be unfunctional, irrelevant, and therefore untruthful. In order to identify truly, you must get as close to the character as you can *without* losing your respect for the character's separate identity as an artistic creation with a definite purpose.

BELIEVABILITY

You must create a character who will do what he must to further the action of his play "believably," that is, *as a logical expression of his very being.* This means that believability comes from the realization of the function and form of your character within the play's structure, not necessarily from seeming "true-to-life" in an everyday sense.

In fact, a character who was "true-to-everyday-life" would seem most *un*believable in any of the great classical plays. Even in a "realistic" play, the expression of character is heightened and selected far beyond everyday life in order to achieve an artistic purpose. So, in portraying a character, your job is *not* necessarily to be true-to-*life* but *always* to be true to your character's *dramatic pursose* and the form of the play in which he appears.

Your understanding of the play's form is an essential part of your understanding of the character, and you empathize with your character with respect for the way in which he expresses himself. You do *not* simply say, "If I were in his place what would I do?" You already know what he *does*, and your analysis of the text has told you much about the way he does it. By filling the outline of the character provided by the text with your own energies, you evoke the quality of *his* experience in *your* consciousness.

Eventually, you empathize fully with your character. His presence becomes "real" and tangible to you, and you have profoundly involved yourself in it. But you have not "lost" yourself, nor have you "lost" him. The good actor does not *become* a character, he *creates* a character. When you *become* a character you have "lost" yourself, and when you lose yourself, you have ceased to be able to make the critical decisions necessary to all art. Yet maintaining the artistic "objectivity" necessary to critical control does *not* necessitate any less imagination, involvement, or "belief" in the character. Rather, it requires the additional skill and discipline to shape and evaluate the results of your empathy with the character.

To be "believable" on stage you must be more than simply alive; you must also be *correctly* alive.

STYLE

"Styles of Acting" is a course usually reserved for advanced students, but a realization of style should be the objective of even the earliest acting experience. One of the most pressing needs in American theatre, especially in the repertory theatres, is for actors who possess an understanding of, and the facility for achieving, appropriate style.

What is style? We often speak of "stylized" plays, meaning nonnaturalistic or highly "artificialized" plays. But style in its broadest sense means much more than that. It is the way in which all the elements of a play have been integrated in a form expressive of the playwright, the age in which he wrote, the social and physical theatrical environment for which he created, and the way in which his play lives for us today. It is, in short, the way in which everything is put together, the cement that bonds all the elements of the play into a unified and expressive whole.

Style, in this sense, is distinguished from *stylization*. *Stylization* implies the imposition of external and artificialized patterns or devices on a play. This is not in itself bad and is sometimes a useful tool of a director's interpretation. But *style* refers to the unique *intrinsic* properties and manner of construction of an individual play. All plays have style, not just "stylized" ones.

Plays of similar types or genres may share strong stylistic similarities. Most Greek tragedies, for example, feature a massive and highly economical form of action. Most Restoration comedies feature highly ornate, verbal humor based upon simile and puns, and extremely complex plots based upon a "sex chase." Since they come from the same milieu, it is not surprising that these plays share a characteristic set of values and emphasize certain qualities of the theatrical experience more or less than other genres. The effect of generic qualities on style is very important. Yet it is dangerous to oversimplify the effect of genre on the style of an individual play, for this kind of thinking leads to the creation of formulas by which certain types of plays "ought" to be performed.

The work of many major playwrights has been mistreated by such oversimplified attitudes about their style: Shakespeare, Shaw, Chekhov, Brecht, and Beckett, to name a few. Such generalized thinking leads to a sameness and a lack of vividness in production. We must always respect the unique and individual demands of a work as interpreted by our director. Our performance should grow organically from our attempt to meet those demands.

Our performance, and the production of which it is a part, have a style of their own. Our objective is to make the style of our performance a direct expression and extension of the style of the play. In other words, we strive to put our performance together on the same principles that provided the stylistic unity of our play.

This means that no *one* acting methodology will serve the needs of all plays. Plays of different generic types are not constructed in the same way; they are based upon different theatrical premises. You can't do Restoration comedy with the same methodology you might use for a play by O'Neill. It would be like teeing off with a putter; you might get somewhere, but you will have created unnecessary obstacles to accuracy and effectiveness.

While there are many common techniques and attitudes involved in all acting, and many similarities for the actor between plays of similar types, still each play presents its own problems and demands its own solutions. *You can't act a style; true style results only from doing the specific job at hand in the way demanded by the form of the play.*

SOCIAL ROLE-PLAYING AND CHARACTERIZATION

In the opening pages of this book, we discussed the similarities between the way in which we all "perform" in everyday life and the basic techniques of stage acting. Now that we have studied some of the many specific demands of stage interpretation and technique which make stage acting more conscious, disciplined, and structured than everyday social acting, we can return to their underlying similarities.

Erving Goffman's book, *The Presentation of Self in Everyday Life*, explores the dramatic process of social acting. He feels that our social performance can be viewed on two levels: the image we consciously desire to project to our audience, and the impressions that, despite our best efforts, they form of us.

> Knowing that an individual is likely to present himself in a light that is favorable to him, the others (to whom he is relating) may divide what they witness into two parts: a part that is relatively easy for the individual to manipulate at will, being chiefly his verbal assertions, and a part in regard to which he seems to have little concern or control, being chiefly derived from the expressions he gives off. The others may then use what are considered to be the ungovernable aspects of his expressive behavior as a check upon the validity of what is conveyed by the governable aspects.[36]

If I appear to be listening to you with the utmost interest and concentration, leaning forward in my chair and straining to catch every word, and yet

---

[36] Goffman, *The Presentation of Self in Everyday Life*, p. 7.

you catch me glancing over your shoulddr or shuffling my foot under my chair, you intuitively compare the information I am trying to *give* you (that I am interested) with the contrary impressions I am unconsciously *giving off* (that I am bored). In this case, you judge me to be insincere; when the information we *give* and that we *give off coincides*, then we are adjudged sincere. Each of us possesses a highly developed faculty for perceiving the unconscious behavior of others, even though such perceptions are themselves often unconscious.

This description of conscious and unconscious behavior during the social performance is useful in describing the stage performance as well. If we have failed to control each aspect of our behavior on stage, including those which are normally beyond conscious control, our audience will perceive behavior that may be contrary to the image we desire to create. Incomplete characterization, lack of concentration, and failure to make strong contact with our fellow actors will all result in behavior that is contrary to our desired impression, and the audience will judge our performance to be unconvincing.

Stanislavski's technique aimed at a strong subjective involvement with the life of the character and was a way of insuring that the actor's own unconscious behavior was utilized in his performance, since the actor's unconscious would supposedly be fully involved with the character. Unfortunately, our unconscious behavior is not very flexible or changeable, since it is habitual and often automatic. If our unconscious behavior *remains* entirely unconscious and is never recognized and evaluated as an element of a purposeful artistic creation, it may work against us. Though in the final creation of our performance, much of what we do has again become unconscious or automatic, at some time in the rehearsal period it must have been consciously evaluated and structured. If, in this way, we stage actors can bring normally unconscious forms of behavior within the realm of our discipline, we will have gained a potent means of controlling our audience's impression of our character and the convincingness of our performance.

Exercise 43: Social and Stage Acting

Part I: Observing Yourself

Using yourself as a subject, observe changes in your everyday behavior from situation to situation. What dramatic devices do you use to reinforce your own sanity by reminding yourself of some consistency behind these performances? You probably refuse to meet some demands made upon you by social role-playing. What are those demands; are any of them similar to demands that may be made upon you on stage? What aspects of the social situation threaten you in the same way that the stage situation does?

Examine also the relationship between your social role-playing and your role-playing on stage. What similarities and what differences are there in the two activites? What skills have you developed socially that will be useful on stage? What inhibitions have you developed socially that will be liabilities on stage?

Are there certain areas of your body, certain types of gestures, which seem further from your conscious control than others? In your own social role-playing, become aware of your "unconscious" behavior. Try to manipulate it.

Part II: Observing Others

Observe others to study the ways in which they project an image of themselves: what similarities are there between this social characterization and one on the stage? What dissimilarities?

Develop your eye and memory for particularly expressive bits of real-life behavior. Do you begin to realize how "stylized" real-life behavior often is? Can we speak of the style of a person in real-life? How might this relate to experiencing the unique qualities of a character in a play, especially a highly "stylized" one?

Try adopting the behavior of people you observe. Does this help you to understand them? Does it give you new experiences and enlarge your own personality? How does this relate to adopting the behavior of a stage character as outlined by a playwright?

WHAT THE ACTOR NEEDS

We can now state a fuller definition of the actor's job: *to fulfill believably his character's dramatic function in a unified, vital, and stylistically accurate stage creation.* The three active ingredients of this definition are FUNCTION, FORM, and VITALITY.

From these three principles, we can state the actor's basic needs, which have provided the content and organization of this book.

1. In order to understand the *function* of your character and the exact quality of action demanded by him, and to know exactly what problems of style a play presents, you must know how to analyze the dramatic text in depth. Just as a musician's ability to perform a composition is dependent upon his music-reading skill and the background he brings to music, so too, you must practice text analysis and equip yourself with a reasonable background in dramatic literature.

2. In order to manifest the *form* of your characterization, you need *mastery of your voice and body.* You will remain a slave to technique until you are in

control of it, able to form concepts and express them without technical restriction.

3. Finally, the *vitality* of your performance is the synthesis of function and form, the focusing of *all* your energy and concentration on the playing of your role. This *role-playing* ability is at once the most basic of your actor's abilities and the most "natural" to you. If your responsiveness as an open and integrated person, your contact with your environment and fellow workers, your mastery of technique, and your understanding of the job to be done are sufficient, your natural energies will be *liberated* and *focused*. It is the liberation and focus of energy that, together, supply vitality.

Group Exercise 10: *Role-Playing*

Using the same scene you prepared for Group Exercise 8, discuss with your partner the ways in which you are each like your characters, and the ways in which you are different.

Discuss how the way in which your characters express themselves and the style of the play demands a different form of behavior than that which is habitual to each of you. On the other hand, what aspects of your natural behavior might be appropriate to the character's style?

Trace your memory to see what experiences and sensations you can remember that relate to those of your character. How might the richness of these experiences be incorporated into your performance? In what ways would they have to be modified?

Finally, rehearse the scene over and over again, stopping to discuss these points, and attempting to project yourself further and further into the character. Check each other's behavior: are you entering into the form demanded by the character? How does each new insight into the character open up new avenues of exploration and experience?

Rehearsal
Discipline

Success is important to all actors, but you must ask yourself what constitutes the true measure of success. Depending on the same attitudes and techniques play after play, no matter how highly developed these techniques may become, can bring only short-term and limited success; the serious actor strives to balance his desire for immediate success with the more important long-range demands of his development as an artist. In short, he approaches each new role, each rehearsal, each performance, not simply with a desire to *succeed* but with a desire to *learn*.

A formal training program offered in the academy, professional school, or university lays the foundation and establishes the future direction of an actor's development, and every serious actor continues to develop and extend his skills with disciplined regularity throughout his lifetime. But there is no real substitute for the valuable experience earned in an honest and intensive utilization of the rehearsal situation. It is in meeting the day-to-day demands of preparing plays for performance and in the performances themselves that the actor finds the fullest source of his development. This is why the actor in a repertory company, preparing a continuous variety of roles, develops his skills much faster than the actor who works only occasionally or in long runs of individual shows.

This "learning by doing" depends, however, upon how well the actor takes advantage of his rehearsal opportunities. Many actors with the chance to work steadily choose to fall deeper and deeper into their own ruts, depending time and again upon proven gimmicks and tricks. Such actors cheat their public and themselves, wasting invaluable opportunities to expand their artistry by honestly working to solve the unique problems of each play they do. It is artistic growth that makes the rehearsal the most important of all the actor's activities. It is not simply a time to learn lines and blocking; its true purpose is to allow the creative ensemble to *explore alternatives* and to *make choices*.

EXPLORATION IN REHEARSAL

The kind of exploration that takes place in rehearsal is not only the individual actor's exploration of character, but also a group exploration of the moments that pass between characters. Therefore, besides making contact with our fellow actors, we must equally trust and make contact with the *moment* itself.

When we say "trust the moment," we mean that in any rehearsal there are a great many unpredictable variables at work, and the ensemble must be receptive to them. Rehearsal is a time of risk; the ensemble must, as a unit, step off into the unknown of the immediate moment. It is not a blind step, and much thought and preparation goes into it; but at some time, we must allow the flow of events driven by real contact between actors to carry us along.

Too often, actors treat rehearsals much as if they were performances, planning in great detail what they mean to do in advance. The director is thrust into the role of moderator, attempting to bring their various prefabricated performances into some kind of peaceful coexistence. The impulse to "succeed" is so strong in most actors that they refuse to risk failure at the very time when such a risk is the first order of business, as it is in rehearsal. No honest exploration is possible under such circumstances.

Of course, a great deal of "homework" must preceed all rehearsal; a great deal of thought and private experimentation should accompany the memorization of lines and other mundane tasks, which the actor must accomplish outside the rehearsal hall. Never should you waste the time of your fellow actors and director by failing to prepare fully for rehearsal. But this private preparation should not result in *decision*. Your prerehearsal homework contemplates the alternatives and prepares you to explore aggressively in concert with your fellows, and mutually to respect and support the explorations of the director and other cast members.

Not all or even many of your rehearsal discoveries will result from conscious experimentation, however; you must have the courage to invite the *happy accident*. Such spontaneous discovery grows only from the receptiveness and responsiveness of each cast member to each other and to the moment.

Rehearsal is exploration, but never *indiscriminate* exploration. Any meaningful exploration has a sense of goal, which directs the outflow of energy and prevents it from degenerating into blind flailing. Even though goals are rarely clear at the outset, and a good bit of the rehearsal process consists of clarifying them, there is usually in the vision of a play as communicated by the director some sense of the direction in which we must head.

Besides being a time of exploration, rehearsal is also a time of decision. The purpose of our exploration is to provide the richest possible basis upon which decisions may be made, to reveal and test as many of the alternatives as possible. But eventually, choices must be made.

MAKING CHOICES

The many choices that must be made during rehearsal cannot be prejudged: we must actually *do* the thing in order to know if it is right or not. One of the most common expressions you will hear during rehearsal is "that sounds like a good idea, let's try it." Then you will hear either "that feels right," or "that doesn't feel right."

"Feeling right" is a good description of how choices are made in the theatre. Your analysis and research in preparation for rehearsal will not usually lead to stage choices, but rather will reveal a wealth of alternatives for exploration. The best knowledge that an actor and his director have of a play comes from actually experiencing it on the stage. Our earlier discussion of the James-Lange theory that emotions grow out of physical actions will suggest what "feeling right" really means. Any action on stage, vocal or physical, will inspire in the receptive actor certain feelings. Since his intellectual conception of his role provides some idea of what he is trying to achieve, he intuitively compares the feelings inspired by specific actions with his conceptual model, and hence makes his choice. Each decision opens up new areas of exploration and often a rehearsal experiment will initiate a sequence of discoveries that expand conception and interpretation.

Such really meaningful discoveries can be made only in the context of the working rehearsal, when the participants are honestly in contact, working as a team toward a common goal. There is a dictum in the theatre that "Acting is Reacting." Each action on stage is a reaction to some previous action and in turn evokes new reactions. The rightness of any action, therefore, will be determined by the way in which it fits into the cause-effect communication between characters. This places even more emphasis upon the directness of the contact between you and your fellow actors, and between you and the environment created by the playwright, since it is in the light of an active give-and-take that all decisions will be made.

At best, the right moment will arise of its own accord, and no one will have any difficulty in recognizing such truth. The best rehearsal environment is one in which the truth can most easily arise. but there is no one way to achieve this. Some plays demand a free experimental approach, while others require methodical technical planning. The actors and their director must decide on the best approach to each particular play. Discoveries cannot be made without some aggressive investigation, and we must initiate the process in a way appropriate to the truth we seek.

Since rehearsal exploration is a dynamic process in which each decision will reflect upon all other decisions, we must decide from moment to moment how completely we ought to be committed to a certain action at a given point of time in the rehearsal process. Some actors wait a long time before making their final choices, and approach their roles warily and flatly in early rehearsals, gradually filling in the full performance. Others produce at performance levels right off, though they maintain enough flexibility to avoid making final choices too soon. You will have to determine your own best approach, in terms of the disposition of the director, your fellow actors, the nature of the play, the length of the rehearsal period, and so on. As a general rule, however, an actor's output of energy should be as high as or higher than performance levels during rehearsals. The actor who lies back and plays the waiting game is usually being unfair to his co-workers, since they depend upon him for their reactions. But this should not force him to make final decisions too soon, commiting himself to insufficiently explored and tested actions.

One way of working (though not the "only" one) is exemplified by Paul Scofield's preparation as King Lear in Peter Brook's production, recorded here in the assistant director's notebook:

First Reading at Stratford

Brook spoke of the play as a mountain whose summit had never been reached. On the way up one found the shattered bodies of other climbers strewn on every side. "Olivier here, Laughton there; it's frightening."

Describing the enormity of the task before us, he gave one of the aptest definitions of the rehearsal process I've ever heard: "The work of rehearsals is looking for meaning and then making it meaningful." To illustrate the extent of this search, he related a short oriental fable about a man whose wife had suddenly disappeared. A neighbor came upon the man sifting sand on a lonely beach, and asked what he was doing. "I have lost my wife," he explained. "I know she is somewhere and therefore have to look for her everywhere."

The day was devoted to a straight readthrough of the play. It was a reading full of conventional verse-speaking; at times robustly acted; at other times, dully mouthed by actors torn between study of the text and performance. Paul Scofield used the reading mainly as a study-session—struggling with the verse like a man trapped in clinging ivy and trying to writhe his way through. One was immediately aware of the actor's resolve and caution. Scofield circled Lear like a wary challenger measuring out an unbeaten opponent and it was apparent from the start that this challenger was a strategist rather than a slugger.

First Dress Rehearsal

Scofield's Lear has slowly begun to emerge. His method is to start from the text and to work backwards. He is constantly testing the verse to see if the sound corresponds with the emotional intention. It is a peculiar method which consciously prods technique so that instinct will be called into play. The Method actor starts with feelings and then adds the externals of voice and movement. Scofield uses externals as a gauge with which to measure the truth of any given speech. He frequently stammers his lines, openly testing inflections and accents, discarding conventional readings not because they are predictable but because they do not tally with an inner sense of verisimilitude.

His concentration is a model to the rest of the company. He even asks for a prompt in character. Only when fumbling for a line does one glimpse the disparity between the man and the character, and then what one sees is a man winding painfully into a Shakespearean fiction. Underlying all the rigor of creative application, one discerns the gentleness of the man himself.[37]

Scofield's method of starting from the text and "working backward" is very close to the approach we have studied here. It is a way to involve "instinct" and the unconscious, without losing the critical control of externals demanded of all good acting.

GETTING ALONG: THE ACTOR AND HIS FELLOWS

Your relationship with your fellow actors must be founded upon trust and mutual respect. It is so out of necessity, as each of your performances is fully dependent on what you give and receive from each other. In the very early stages of rehearsal, before close rapport has been established within the company, it is especially important that each actor make the act of faith to work together toward the defining of goals with respect, trust, good humor, and a generous heart. Later on, as ideas begin to form themselves and decisions come closer, we must avoid a rigidity of attitude that prevents the organic development of a cohesive group interpretation.

Perhaps the most dangerous rigidity is exemplified by the actor who becomes an apologist for his character, arguing from the character's point of view as if every scene were "his." Group interpretation can be ruined by actors who insist upon adopting their character's point of view at the expense of the actor-craftsman's view of the play as an artistic whole.

---

[37] Charles Marowits, "Lear in Rehearsal," (in the program of the 400th anniversary tour of the U.S.) *Royal Shakespeare Company in King Lear/ The Comedy of Errors* (Stratford-Upon-Avon, England: Herald Press, 1964), p. 3.

On the other hand, we do a great disservice to our director and fellow actors, and ourselves, if out of a false desire to get along, we fail to express ourselves honestly. An actor who is *too* pliable is as destructive as one who is too rigid. Your ideas will be appreciated by your ensemble if they are presented in a reasoned, timely, and respectful fashion. One word of warning: Your director must be the center of all company communication. Your feelings and ideas are best expressed directly to him, not to fellow actors in private conversations. A show must have only one director, though everyone connected with it must feel the responsibility of providing the director with ideas that may be of value.

THE ACTOR AND HIS DIRECTOR

Each director has a characteristic way of working, and it is part of the actor's job to help the director develop the most effective channel of communication with himself and with the company. Actors and directors are co-workers, not master and slave. The actor and his director, though they share many responsibilities, have essentially different functions, which are interdependent and co-equal. The director's responsibility is first to the over-all patterning of the play as a theatrical experience; the actor's responsibility is to bring his role to life so as to best contribute to that patterning.

There are many ways in which these responsibilities overlap and where compromise will be necessary. In his effort to shape the experience of the play, the director will inevitably need to determine certain specific actions or character traits. At the same time, the actor, in his struggle to bring the character to life, must receive from his director an environment conducive to the growth of that life.

The actor, intimately involved with the life of his character, possesses insights into the life of that character, which are denied the director. At the same time, the director, with his overview and special position as the source of interpretation, has an objective point of view unavailable to any actor. In an effective working relationship, each will respect and value the special insights of the other and seek to join their points of view to the best possible advantage.

Even at the best, however, there are times when insoluble disagreements will occur. At such times, the actor must remember that the director has assumed public responsibility for the audience's experience of the play. On his side, the actor has assumed public responsibility for the portrayal of his character within the context established by the director's interpretation, and once the interpretation has been clarified, it is the actor's responsibility to find the best possible means of implementing it. Therefore, it is ultimately the director's function to evaluate *what* the actor does, and the actor's job to find *how* best to do it. They are equally creative artists, the director being an artist of *what*, and the actor being an artist of *how*.

THE ACTOR AND THE PLAYWRIGHT

Some playwrights have (like Strindberg) congratulated actors on creating characters who improved the original. But even more playwrights have (like Chekhov) been shocked at finding the actor's creation to bear little relation to their original. Some few playwrights (like Tennessee Williams) have occasionally permitted actors and directors to make changes in their basic conception of a play. Others (like Edward Albee) have insisted that their plays remain uncut and unchanged. Still others (like Ionesco) have allowed portions of their plays to grow out of a "group-write" improvisational situation.

The playwright, as we know him today, is a recent invention. He seems unfortunately isolated from the theatre for which he writes. But in most great ages of theatre, playwrights were working members of the producing units for which they wrote. Most serious playwrights have made an attempt to involve themselves in the day-to-day working of their production unit and to gain practical stage experience, rather than remaining literary artists who happen to write in a dramatic format. Theatrical chain-of-command has made this difficult, if not impossible, for most playwrights to do on a professional level, and our theatre has suffered for it. The emerging repertory companies and other organizations, usually with the help of grants-in-aid, are beginning to bring the playwright back into the working ensemble.

Most of the time, however, we do not have the benefit of the author's presence, nor even the benefit of any clear idea about the author's intention as expressed apart from the text itself. Under these conditions, it is often assumed that the director will take the playwright's part, and through his own exhaustive analysis of the play will discover all necessary information that the author might otherwise supply. Unfortunately some directors are guilty of using texts as mere vehicles for their own creation.

In the other extreme, some directors force themselves and their actors to conform so rigidly to their notion of the author's intention that the actor finds it impossible to make a creative contribution to the production. Many academic directors have such a pronounced desire for anonymity, regarding themselves only as unobtrusive middlemen for the author, that they exalt drabness and equanimity to the level of theatrical virtues. In all this the actor has the difficult task of maintaining his primary responsibility to the authority of the director, without abdicating his sense of respect for the original.

HONING THE PERFORMANCE

The actor often expends more energy during rehearsals than he does in performance, and he generally expends less and less energy as performances continue after opening. This is not because he begins doing his part mechanically without thought or feeling, but because he penetrates deeper and deeper to the essence of the part. As this happens, unessential detail begins to fall away.

As the actor grows in proficiency, his energy output will also be economized. No matter how difficult the thing is, the seasoned veteran usually makes it look easy, because he knows what is essential and what is not. Our performance is usually made more effective by so economizing it as to distill it to its essential detail. This focuses the audience's attention clearly on the details that contribute most directly to the vitality of the play as a whole. This "natural attrition" of unessential detail usually occurs during a run under pressure of audience response, though there is no reason why natural attrition cannot be at work during rehearsals as well. A dual process with new actions being explored and established ones being distilled to their essence can be achieved simultaneously.

EVALUATING OUR CHOICES

Whether we adopt externals, or allow them to be generated out of interior states, or do both at once, we must continue to exercise critical judgement of the results. If we rely only on our intuition and feelings, we have no adequate objective judgment of the appropriateness of our externals. On the other hand, if we judge ourselves entirely by externals, we are probably being so objective that we become dangerously estranged from the inner life of the character. The only alternative, and the one practised by most actors, is to reserve one level of consciousness which remains "distanced," while on other levels there is a profound identification with the character.

This similtaneous operation of various levels of our consciousness is an everyday phenomenon. At all but moments of extreme passion, we have some sense of objective self-awareness. In the same way, the actor reserves a portion of his consciousness to evaluate the appropriateness and effectiveness of the character's behavior in relation to his over-all dramatic purpose. He depends on his director to supply a truly objective viewpoint during rehearsals, and in performance his reading of the subtle reactions (or 'feedback') of the audience supplements his own critical faculty.

A NOTE ON AUDITIONS

Finally, we must discuss the point at which the actor's job usually begins. Auditions are a painful but necessary part of the actor's job, and if it is any consolation, directors dislike auditions even more than do actors. The initial casting of a play is one of the most influential steps in the determination of interpretation, and yet the director must make these crucial decisions when he has only minimal acquaintance with his actors' work. Most directors have their own audition techniques, some of which can be rather disarming.

Most directors ask the actor to perform a few speeches of different types, and the actor should have at least three or four carefully chosen and prepared audition scenes, including comedy and tragedy, poetic and modern styles. About two minutes is a good length for each. The speeches should be chosen to demonstrate your abilities to the best advantage, and it is wise to avoid the standard audition speeches. It is difficult to evaluate an actor's work, or even to listen to him, when he is doing the sixteenth identical speech from *Richard III* that day.

Other directors prefer to have actors read scenes from the play at hand. Time, in this circumstance, allows only minimal preparation. Some actors can give polished cold readings with only a few moments work, but directors are usually suspicious of this; many times these slick cold-readers fail to develop much beyond their initial reading. On the other hand, some competent actors are so slow of study and such late-bloomers that they are at a hopeless disadvantage in most audition situations. Directors therefore are as much interested in your past experience and reliable references about your work as they are in the immediate audition, and you should be prepared to provide this information in an organized and attractive resumé and composite picture.

Auditions will be much more enjoyable if you approach them without a sense of competitiveness, but rather as an opportunity to communicate your potential to the director. Remember that the auditioners are under even greater pressure than you, since there is a great deal riding on the wisdom of their choice. Your objective should be to assist them in making their choice honestly. Whether or not you are cast or get the particular role you wanted, auditions challenge you to face great pressure with integrity and a willing spirit. Auditions do not test your artistry so much as they test your usefulness to the director for the specific task at hand. Moreover, the opinion formed of you at an audition may be important at some future time; it is therefore important that you honestly present your best abilities and avoid falsifying yourself for the sake of the particular instance. The question young actors most often ask about an audition is, "What do they want?" A much better question would be, "How can I best show them what I am?"

LOOKING FORWARD

This book has presented only a part of the basic technique that a well-equipped actor needs, but it has attempted to lay a firm foundation for future work. As I warned in the introduction, we are stopping short of the most important step in the student actor's development, the beginning of scene work aimed at the realization of character; hopefully you now possess most (certainly not all) of the skills needed to take that step firmly and with a strong sense of direction.

As you do, you will discover that much more remains to be learned, especially about the operation of character. The analysis we have studied here has dealt with the individual details that go to make up the larger structure of the role and of the play. We have not yet attacked that larger structure, and that should be your next order of business. The creation of an effective characterization demands a synthesis of the skills and detail studied here, a synthesis caused by the pressure of an over-all artistic conception of the role. The accurate formation of such a concept depends on the understanding of detail, and expression of concept depends on specific technical skills, but only the power of the concept itself can give shape, meaning, and vitality to our performance.

The ability to form such a concept will begin to develop best under the pressure of practical work. In classroom scene work, supervised and critiqued by a teacher concerned with your continuing development, and later in preparing roles for performance, the experience of attempting to solve specific acting problems in specific instances will provide the impetus to expand continually your technique and analytical skills throughout the remainder of your acting life.